THE Confident Retirement JOURNEY

THE **Confident Retirement** JOURNEY

YOUR PERSONAL & FINANCIAL ROAD MAP

by Ron Kelemen

Confident Vision Press, LLC
Salem, Oregon

Ron Kelemen is a fee-only CERTIFIED FINANCIAL PLANNER™ licensee with The H Group, Inc. in Salem, Oregon. The opinions expressed in this book are those of Ron Kelemen, CFP® and do not necessarily reflect those of The H Group, Inc. and its other advisory associates. The purpose of this book is to provide a broad overview of issues related to retirement planning, which may not be relevant to all individuals. Therefore, no reader should assume that this book serves as the receipt of, or a substitute for, personalized advice from Mr. Kelemen, The H Group, Inc., Confident Vision Press, LLC, or any other investment professional. The contents of this book should not be construed as legal or tax advice. While every effort has been made to provide accurate information, the author makes no representation as to its completeness or accuracy. The strategies, statistics, and concepts of this book may become outdated by the passage of time. All economic information is historical and not indicative of future results.

The Confident Retirement Journey™, Your Confident Retirement Journey™, The Confident Retirement Journey Approach™, The Confident Retirement Journey Balance Sheet™, and The Confident Retirement Journey Expense Analysis™ are trademarks of Confident Vision Press, LLC. The Second-Half Vision Focuser™, The Retirement Readiness Process™, The Confident Legacy Vision®, and The Confident Retirement Vision® are trademarks of Kelemen Advisory Associates, LLC.

Published by Confident Vision Press, LLC.
Salem, Oregon

www.ConfidentRetirementJourney.com

© 2013 by Ron Kelemen
All rights reserved.

Printed in the United States of America
ISBN 978-0-578-13054-5

For Kathy and Mary
Two of my best decisions in life

Contents

Preface

We are awash with so much financial data and information these days that it is difficult to know what to believe, and even more difficult to take action. How do you make sense of the countless books, newsletters, magazine articles, blogs, newscasts, commercials, and newspaper advice columns that surround us daily? Some of that information eventually becomes useful knowledge, but much of it does not become wisdom. Why? Because so much of this information is generated by well-meaning and often credentialed people who have little or no practical experience advising clients on a daily basis. It's one thing to talk about fees, performance, tax provisions, and investment strategies. Anybody can write about those, as I have. It's quite another to console a tearful widow, tell an anxious couple they can't afford to retire next year, or be proudly introduced at a client's retirement party.

Over the past thirty-two years, I have gained practical wisdom advising clients "from the trenches," helping them navigate the complexities of personal finance and investment management. I've seen what works and what doesn't work, what positive things can result from planning, and the need to help clients adjust as they go through life. I've shared these insights in my quarterly newsletter for twenty-one years and in a monthly column for local medical societies for sixteen years.

What worries me is that so many people are either clueless about what they need to do for a secure and fulfilling retirement or they are confused by friends, relatives, advertisements, and financial advice in the media and do nothing about it. So, after hearing many times from clients, peers, and acquaintances, "Wow, Ron, that's a good article. You should write a book on the topic," I decided it was time.

What follows, then, isn't a compilation of articles but rather an organized narrative of how I would advise friends or clients about what they need to do to become confident about their retirement, from both a personal and a financial point of view. Whether or not you work with a financial advisor, I hope this book gives you the confidence you need to enjoy a secure and fulfilling second half of your life.

Acknowledgments

You are reading this because of the rich fabric of clients, colleagues, allied professionals, strategic partners, team members, friends, family members, and opportunities that have been a huge part of my life. They are too numerous to name individually, but my sincere thanks to all of them for their support and encouragement over the years.

However, a few people close to me deserve special recognition. Kathy, my best friend and wife of thirty-six years, is the CFO of our practice and my sounding board. Her support enables me to do what I do. In 1995, Mary Way, CPA, CFP® joined my practice. That was the second-best decision of my life, as we have become strong and trusted teammates together, complementing each other's strengths. In 2011, Larry Hanslits, CFP® merged his practice with ours. I have collaborated with him on highly complex planning cases ever since 1985, and it is a joy to have him on the team and as a financial partner. And our team wouldn't be "Team Salem" and the Salem Area Chamber of Commerce's 2011 Small Business of the Year without the support of Debbie Renggli, Lani Moore, our new associate Brenna Baucum, our portfolio managers Ryan Long and Jen Plett, and our associates at The H Group, Inc. They make me look good and free me up to meet with clients and write. Special thanks go to Ryan and Jen who compiled much of the historical investment data for the charts. And to Todd Sakoda, who helped with compliance issues.

We became a real team in 1995 when I started attending the quarterly workshops of Strategic Coach® and organizing my practice around its principles. I want to thank Dan Sullivan, its founder, for his structure, tools, and wisdom. They have immeasurably helped us to better serve our clients and support them as they think about their futures. Some of that thinking is woven into the chapters that follow.

Finally, it takes more than a manuscript to make a book happen. So, my thanks go to Brenna Baucum, Martha Lewis and Brandon Conn with In House Graphics, Kari Filburn with Line by Line Copyediting, Edwin Peterson, Natalie Brown, and Your Town Press for turning this manuscript into what you are reading now.

Introduction

Let's face it. In today's social and economic environment, it takes confidence to retire. It wasn't always this way. The parents of today's baby boomers could rely on defined benefit pensions, limited investment and savings options, Social Security, and rather narrow concepts of retirement. In a perverse way, they could also "rely" upon lower life expectancies, thus requiring less in retirement savings.

Not so today. Baby boomers and their children are bombarded with financial news, investment choices, less predictable income sources, many competing visions of retirement, rapidly changing technology, and the prospects of living much longer than their parents.

So, rather than something to be anticipated with joy, retirement is becoming a source of stress for many near and current retirees. According to a poll by American Demographics, 41 percent of retirees say retirement was a difficult adjustment. By contrast, only 12 percent of newlyweds saw marriage as a difficult adjustment, and only 23 percent thought becoming parents was difficult.[1] I can attest to these percentages, having helped many people get through this transition over the years. Embarking on the retirement journey takes skill, good counsel, and a lot of money. But above all, it requires an attitude of confidence and a sense of vision.

I want this book to give you the sense of confidence that you can thrive in and enjoy your retirement journey. And what is the destination of this journey? It is simply to find fulfillment and financial security for the second half of your life. It's not an end point but rather a process. I'll share some confidence-building strategies my team and I have developed over the past thirty-plus years of advising clients. These will help you to create your own retirement vision and take specific action steps, confident that you are making progress in a world full of distracting financial noise. Let the journey begin!

The Retirement Landscape

Toto, I've a feeling we're not in Kansas anymore.
— Dorothy, *The Wizard of Oz*

Like any trip, it's usually a good idea to make some basic preparations and have the lay of the land in mind before starting out. There are dangers and opportunities on this retirement journey, but that's what makes it an adventure. Our routes and the length of our trip may vary, but we all have six landmarks in common. Let's take a look at them before we begin the journey.

Landmark 1: The 3.5 Phases of Retirement

Most preretirees intuitively sense that retirement isn't the same from start to end. So, to get a handle on this continuum, think of retirement as three phases, as first described in 1998 by Michael Stein.[2]

Phase 1: The Active Phase or "Go-Go"

These are the early years of retirement when you have the health and energy to travel and maintain an active lifestyle. In Michael's words, this is "a second childhood without parental supervision."

Phase 2: The Passive Phase or "Go Slow"

This is a time when it's just harder to get around and do a lot of active things. It's a time of quiet pleasures. Quite often, this coincides with more time with grandchildren and great-grandchildren.

Phase 3: The Final Phase or "No Go"

This is a time when your mobility, cognition, and health become dominating issues. It could mean assisted living or nursing care, forfeiting driving privileges, and staying close to home.

Phase 0.5: The Trial Phase

For some people, I would add this additional phase. This is for pre-retirees who have the ability to phase into a full retirement, to take more vacation time, or to structure their work weeks as they approach a "cold-turkey" retirement.

Landmark 2: Life Expectancy

These three-and-a-half phases vary in length among couples and individuals. Collectively, though, the most significant development affecting the retirement landscape today isn't Social Security, pension reform, or the stock market but rather that we are all living longer. How long can we expect to be retired? Let's take a look.

According to the 2000 Annuity Mortality Table, a seventy-year-old female has a life expectancy of an additional 18.81 years.[3] This means that the *group* will live to an *average age* of 88.81, not necessarily any particular individual. Think of it as a 50-50 proposition—half will die before that age and half will die after that age.

And for sixty-five-year-olds, the Society of Actuaries estimates the average male has a life expectancy of an additional fifteen years; females, seventeen.[4] The following are more statistics for men who are sixty-five today:

- 70 percent will survive to 80
- 52 percent will survive to 85
- 31 percent will survive to 90
- 13 percent will survive to 95

And here are more numbers for women who are sixty-five today:

- 74 percent will survive to 80
- 59 percent will survive to 85
- 39 percent will survive to 90
- 20 percent will survive to 95

But from a retirement planning aspect, it gets very expensive when planning for couples. Think of yourselves as an actuarial group of two individuals. If you are both sixty-five-year-old nonsmokers, one of you has a chance of the following:

- 50 percent chance of living to age 92
- 30 percent chance of living to age 96
- 20 percent chance of living to age 98
- 10 percent chance of living to age 101

Wow, hard to believe, isn't it? But look around. We have client couples, widows, and widowers well into those ages. You probably know of friends and family members in that range as well.

So, your retirement may last much longer and cost more than you expect. This is a danger that can become a huge opportunity: you could be retired longer than you worked. If you are financially prepared and take care of your health, you might have the time to enjoy a long and fulfilling journey. This changes everything.

Landmark 3: Inflation

I became passionate about financial planning because of my dad. In 1976, at age fifty-five, he was forced into retirement after thirty years with the same company. "No problem," he explained. "I've got a pension of $300 per month, and I'll start Social Security at sixty-two." At that time, it was very doable, especially given his frugal lifestyle, some savings, and a paid-off mortgage. But shortly after that, we experienced nearly a decade of double-digit inflation. He eventually had to return to work selling real estate well into his seventies to make ends meet. When he died in 1999, his $300-per-month pension had the purchasing power of only $102.[5]

We are enjoying relatively low inflation in 2013. But historically, inflation has averaged 3 percent over the past eighty-five years and 4.14 percent over the past fifty years.[6] The Bureau of Labor Statistics (BLS) has been tinkering with the Consumer Price Index (CPI) since 1983.[7] In its CPI calculations, the BLS now accounts for the fact that people are able to substitute one product for another when faced with rapid price increases, such as eating burgers when steak prices soar. However, if you don't make a substitution, your annual cost of living will increase faster than the official CPI. There are some things that you just can't substitute, such as medical expenses, which typically rise much faster than the official CPI.

Here's your takeaway: even at only a 3 percent inflation rate, prices double every twenty-four years. Another way of looking at it is that $1,000 would be worth only $500. That's a real loss, and far more insidious than a 10–20 percent stock market swing in any given year. This is the Rule of 72 in action: in order to estimate how quickly an asset or price doubles, simply take the assumed growth or inflation rate and divide that into 72. At 4 percent, for example, prices double every eighteen years, and about every fourteen years at 5 percent.

If you started a cross-country road trip with only enough gas money at today's prices, you could become stranded if gas prices spiked. Likewise, to be confident about your retirement journey, you need to be prepared for inflation.

Landmark 4: Social Security

For most Americans, Social Security is an important cornerstone of retirement, more so for those with low retirement incomes and assets. However, it was never intended to be a sole source of income for retirees. The Social Security Administration reports that the average payment in 2013 will be $1,261 for all retired workers and $2,048 for all retired couples.[8] But even if you earn a high income and have projected retirement living expenses exceeding $20,000 per month, Social Security can keep you on the road and help minimize withdrawals from your investment portfolio. If, over the past three decades, you earned the maximum taxable Social Security wage base ($113,700 in 2013, but as low as $32,400 in 1982), you could receive the following income:

- $1,912 per month at age sixty-two
- $2,550 per month at age sixty-six
- $3,366 per month at age seventy[9]

If you have a spouse, he or she could earn the greater of half of that, depending upon his or her earnings history. And, by the way, these numbers do not include cost-of-living adjustments (COLAs), which make them more valuable over time.

The future of Social Security has certainly been in the news these days, with some inflammatory and fear-inducing sound bites. But know this: Congress and the Board of Trustees of the Social Security Trust Funds agree that current benefits *can* continue without changes for the next twenty years.[10] That is because payroll taxes and redemptions of the special Social Security Treasury Bonds are sufficient until then. Unless changes are made, the trust fund will be depleted by 2033, and the system will rely on just payroll taxes. At that time, benefits would need to drop to 77 percent of their current level.[11]

I'll be discussing Social Security strategies in chapter 6. Meanwhile, keep a confident attitude about Social Security, and start thinking about claiming your benefits later to extend your journey—much like a series of monthly filling stations down the road.

Landmark 5: Health

I don't have any evidence for this, but I think that people who take care of their health are generally more confident about life. If you've ever had an injury or gotten sick, you know how that can destroy your outlook. The length and quality of your journey is going to depend upon your health, wealth, and relationships. The retirees we work with want to extend the active phase of their retirement for as long as possible. However, not all of us will be so lucky—we're all just one injury or life-threatening disease away from a shortened or not-so-fulfilling retirement. Some things we can control, some we can't.

And that's where money and health insurance enter your retirement picture. For the past ten years, the Fidelity Benefits Consulting Group has estimated projected medical expenses of retirees. In 2002, Fidelity calculated that a couple, each at age sixty-five and without employer or pension health insurance, could expect to pay about $160,000 over their retirement years. Fidelity's estimate for 2013? Try a whopping $220,000 on for size![12] These costs are over and above what Medicare pays. Of course, this is just an estimate based on the laws, costs, and programs as they exist today. Your longevity and health can also affect the results for better or worse. Either way, you need to be confident that you can handle these expenses on your journey.

Medicare, as we know it today, is an important piece of your retirement safety net. Given the rise in medical costs, the sheer number of boomers entering retirement, and the longevity of today's seniors, it is no wonder the system will be facing problems within the next ten years. Changes will certainly need to be made to keep it viable. But—as politicians floating trial balloons for solutions are learning—it won't be going away. Instead, it is likely that we will all be required to assume more financial responsibility. This can take the form of co-pays, deductibles, nonallowed expenses, and means-testing for high-income recipients. Regardless of costs, many new retirees find

Medicare to be a confidence booster and a better deal than what they had before retirement.

You may not develop an expensive medical condition, but perhaps you will lose your ability to function well on your own (hopefully after you've had a long and fulfilling Phase 1 and Phase 2). The US Department of Health and Human Services reports that people who reach age sixty-five have a 40 percent chance of entering a nursing home. About 10 percent of them will remain there five years or more.[13] But these are probabilities for sixty-five-year-olds as a group. Your individual odds of needing long-term care are either 100 percent or 0 percent: either you will need it or you won't. If you do, the costs and damage to your assets could be catastrophic. There are other forms of long-term care besides nursing homes, such as assisted living or in-home care, but no matter what, they are all expensive. You can either self-insure with enough assets or buy some "trip insurance" (e.g., a long-term care policy) so that you don't have to reserve a lot of assets for something you may not need.

Landmark 6: Money and Investments

By now, after seeing the first five landmarks on the map, you can easily guess that retirement is expensive. Period. The only income for your twenty-, thirty-, or forty-year journey is what you send ahead in the form of investments, pension credits, part-time employment, and Social Security taxes.

Your money and health are the two most important drivers of a confident retirement journey. If you take care of them, they can take care of you. Your money cannot retire when you do—it needs to work hard both now and well into the future. Yes, it may occasionally suffer on-the-job injuries during financial downturns, but your job is to get it back to work.

Money and investing have become far more complicated than when our parents and grandparents approached retirement. Most had defined benefit pensions, Social Security, passbook savings accounts, and cash-value life insurance. A few ventured into stocks, bonds, and mutual funds.

When I first started my practice in 1981, *Money* magazine was relatively new. There were no TV channels dedicated to financial news 24/7. The Internet didn't exist. Back then, the challenge was getting information and being able to act upon it. It was expensive, slow, and always filtered through intermediaries. Today, we are awash in financial information. The challenge is to avoid overreacting to it or becoming paralyzed by it. I'll share some techniques to deal with all this "financial noise" in chapter 7. One big change I have noticed among my clients, and the public in general, is that we've all become far more aware of and obsessed with money. This is for several reasons:

- Globalization of the financial markets
- The Great Recession
- National debt and deficit issues
- Volatile stock market
- Low interest rates
- Depressed real estate prices
- High and persistent unemployment
- Constant political talk about the economy
- Realization that money—or the lack of it—really does matter

These have all converged to make us anxious about our financial future. We need to accept this, put it into proper perspective, and not let our thoughts about money destroy our retirement confidence.

So, this sums up some key landmarks to navigate in retirement. Let's begin planning our journey!

Your Road Map Action Items

1. Get a pad of paper and a pencil to make notes as you go through the next chapters.
2. Have a simple calculator handy to help you make basic calculations for the worksheets ahead.

What's Your Retirement Vision?

*If you don't know where you're going,
you'll wind up somewhere else.*
—Yogi Berra

Freedom. Travel. Hobbies. Time with grandchildren. No deadlines. Less stress. Volunteer work. Slower pace. Part-time work. Doing only what you want to do.

These are but a few thoughts that come to mind when we think of the term *retirement*. What is your definition of retirement? If you don't have a clear vision and a plan to make it happen, retirement and what it represents may remain an elusive dream. It could be like a road trip without a destination in mind. Spontaneity can be good, and things just might turn out okay. But then again, you might miss some worthwhile sights, or you might run out of gas along the way.

Why is creating a retirement vision so hard for many people? I think it is because it is "scary-exciting," the big white board for the second half of your life. And it might involve making changes right now to organize your life and finances in a way that supports this vision for the rest of your life. Hopefully, this chapter will make it easier for you to create your vision thoughtfully and thoroughly. It all starts with a few broad questions that beget more questions. You will probably need to revisit your answers often in the hours and months ahead. So get out a yellow pad or tablet computer, and put your answers in writing.

Why Retire?

Retirement is built on the assumption that leisure is more fulfilling than work. For many people, especially those who enjoyed their careers, that assumption goes against their need to be productive. That is why we see financially comfortable people working well into their seventies and beyond. Work can also provide important mental stimulation and a social outlet with a network of friends, colleagues, and customers. Others see it as part of their identity. When asked what they do for a living, they answer with a verb: "I *am* a (doctor, lawyer, teacher, etc.)." It could very well be that your idea of a fulfilling retirement is some work or volunteer activity—not because you *have* to, but because you *want* to.

Some people view retirement as a solution to their unhappiness at work. They are running *away* from something instead of *to* something. If you think that this is your situation, make a list of what you like and don't like and why. It might be that you have more likes than dislikes, but your dislikes overshadow the good parts. In that case, *how can you change your work situation so that it is more sustainable and enjoyable?* Not everybody has the luxury of this option, but if you do, give it some serious thought. My team and I have seen examples where clients made some simple tweaks to their job tasks or work schedules and developed a completely new attitude around work and retirement. And, of course, their retirement became more financially secure as a nice side benefit. This could be considered Phase 0.5, mentioned in chapter 1.

To better help you discover your retirement vision, answer the following four questions and complete worksheet 2.1.

Four Big Questions

1. What Are the Most Important Things You Would Like to Accomplish between Now and Retirement?

Some people want to retire because they have a lot of relatively short-term personal projects they want to complete. Have you ever had an unfinished project? You know, the half-cleaned garage, the unfinished quilt? Or how about a half-baked cake? Well, what about those in your work life? Perhaps you have a monumental project that's been a big part of your work. Perhaps you want to make certain that you have developed a deep bench of successors. Whatever it is, you can't launch into retirement on good terms with yourself and those you are leaving behind without closure. Finishing what we start gives us a sense of pride and accomplishment.

2. What Are the Most Important Things You Would Like to Accomplish between Retirement and the End of Your Life?

This is the BIG question, the big white board, the big map across the kitchen table. The answers might be so exciting that they dwarf my other questions. The best way to tackle this is to start with the end in mind, then break it down into bite-size benchmarks. Think of it as a multidimensional bucket list that includes not only money and the proverbial notches in your belt but the kind of person you wanted to be. Imagine that near the end, you are looking back on your life. What are the key things that would lead you to say, "I had a good life"?

Many of our clients have found it helpful to use the following worksheet for each of these themes.

Worksheet 2.1 The Second-Half Vision Focuser™

Your Life Goals for Your Second Half

Today's date:_____

Theme: _____

(Accomplishments, Health, Spiritual Goals, Relationships, Financial)

What are the most important things related to this theme that I want to accomplish between now and the end of my life?

	Lifetime date (age _____)
1.	
2.	
3.	
4.	
5.	
6.	
7.	
8.	
9.	
10.	

Ten-year benchmark date	
1.	
2.	
3.	
4.	
5.	
6.	

One-year benchmark date	
1.	
2.	
3.	

Three-month benchmark date	
1.	
2.	
3.	

Three-year benchmark date	
1.	
2.	
3.	
4.	
5.	

One-month benchmark date	
1.	
2.	
3.	

Since some of these categories are interrelated, some clients use just one consolidated—but often expanded—sheet to map out their vision and update it regularly. The important thing is to create measurable benchmarks, or destinations. If, for example, you put "well-traveled" as an end-of-life specification, what does that mean? What are some top destinations or adventures on your bucket list? Approximately when do you want to go to each of them?

These aren't easy questions. They may take time, and your answers will evolve. However, if this exercise doesn't put the last half to one-third of your life into focus, not much else will. You might look at your list and be so excited by all that you want to accomplish that you want to retire today, if financially possible. Good for you—that's a great start. You have your retirement vision with the map on the kitchen table. Now it's just a matter of working out your itinerary.

But if you are like many people, it will take more thought, planning, and preparation. You don't just arrive at your destination with your bucket list checked off. As one of my clients said, "You don't become a good golfer or steelhead fisherman the day you retire—it takes practice." My point is this: why wait until you are retired to begin your journey? Start working on some of your destinations now.

3. What Would Be Your "Perfect Day" in Each of the 3.5 Phases of Retirement?

You might need to break this down into weeks or seasons:

- What will you be doing?
- What will you have?
- Where will you be?
- When will you be there?
- With whom?

4. What about Your Spouse or Significant Other?

- How do your answers compare?

- Do your visions match?
- Can you stand to be around each other twenty-four hours a day?

This area can be very challenging if your ages are significantly different, or if one of you wants to keep working. And think of this: you may have married each other for better or worse, but probably not for lunch every day!

At its essence, retirement is all about the rest of your life, which is going to go by too quickly. Why squander it and let important things slip away? Perhaps you noticed that none of the above questions specifically mentioned money. Yes, some of your dreams—such as travel—will require money, but you first need to have the travel dream to give your money a purpose (and to know how much money you will need). All too often, my team and I have seen clients who retire early or without a vision return to work after a year or two. They got tired of golf every day, did their cross-country trip, or didn't feel useful. They didn't need the money, but they needed a purpose and social connections. This chapter is all about helping you find that purpose for the rest of your life. It is the most important chapter of this book.

Your Road Map Action Items

1. If you are still working, make a list of what you like and dislike about your work. What can you modify to make your job more sustainable and enjoyable?
2. Define your retirement vision by answering the questions presented in this chapter.
3. Complete The Second-Half Vision Focuser™ (worksheet 2.1).

Ron Kelemen

Where Are You Now?

All progress begins by telling the truth.
—Dan Sullivan, Founder of Strategic Coach®

The first thing most people search for when looking at a map is their current location or starting point. Planning your retirement journey is no different. How realistic are your plans, based on where you are today? Do you have adequate provisions? How far will they take you? Are you really confident about that? To be sure, ask yourself the following questions:

1. Will you have enough income from a mix of your savings and other sources, such as Social Security or part-time work?
2. Will you be able to spend more in your earlier retirement years while you still have your health and the energy to do things?
3. Will you have enough resources should your health change or should you need long-term care?
4. Will you be able to weather financial storms, boomerang children, or aging parents?

Apparently, not many people feel that confident about their retirement. According to the Employee Benefit Research Institute's *2013 Retirement Confidence Survey*, only 51 percent of the respondents felt very or somewhat confident that they would have enough money to live comfortably throughout their retirement years. Those with high debts, health issues, and wage compression felt even less confident.[14]

But among those who felt confident, is this confidence warranted? A 2012 study by the Schwartz Center for Economic Policy Analysis looked at retirement savings from the 2010 census, particularly *near retirees,* defined as those individuals age fifty to sixty-four. The results were not pretty. Those households in the top quartile (greater than an income of $100,764) had a median retirement plan balance of only $133,404. The other quartiles had far lower balances.[15]

I'll get into estimating your retirement income in more detail in chapter 4, but assuming a generous 5 percent distribution rate, this $133,404 translates into $6,670 per year. By my "back-of-the-napkin" calculations, it takes over $2 million of capital to replace that $100,764 of household income. If Social Security were included in the mix, perhaps $1.4 million is needed.

Getting a Grip on Your Net Worth

Time and again, we see prospective clients lumping all of their assets together, thinking, "Gee, my net worth is $_____. I could retire on that." Well, not quite. What really matters is which of your assets can actually produce a sustainable, inflation-adjusted income. Your RV, vacation home, or art collection can't do that, unless you are willing to sell them off. Few people actually do, especially with art and collectables. The same holds with your residence. Some people really are downsizing, but many of them are downsizing in size only, not fair market value.

The Confident Retirement Journey Approach™ to Looking at Your Net Worth

To figure out how to reach your retirement vision, you need to know where you stand today. That involves two key assessments: your assets and your liabilities. Think about your assets and liabilities using The Confident Retirement Journey Approach™, which means dividing your assets into two categories: *Financial Independence Assets* and *lifestyle assets*. Financial Independence Assets are everything that you are willing to sell and convert to an income stream *today*. Lifestyle assets are things you need now and in the future for basic necessities and enjoyment. This could include your home, vehicles, toys, etc.

Yes, maybe someday, you might sell the vacation home, large residence, Picasso, or boat, but it's not classified as a Financial Independence Asset until you actually do. Again, we have observed many clients over the years that had good intentions, but they became too attached to their lifestyle or to the asset to actually convert it. Or, in the case of the 2008–2012 collapse of the housing market, large homes couldn't be sold, and home equity evaporated.

By the way, the process works in reverse. The next time you purchase an asset, ask yourself whether it is a true Financial Independence Asset or a lifestyle asset in disguise, which you have no honest intention of selling. This may help curb certain lifestyle purchases that cut into your ability to build solid Financial Independence Assets.

So with these thoughts in mind, clearly divide your net worth statement into two categories:

1. Financial Independence Assets and liabilities
2. Lifestyle assets and liabilities

Worksheet 3.1 The Confident Retirement Journey Balance Sheet™

Type	Assets	Liabilities	Difference
Financial Independence *Possessions that can generate cash flow*			
Lifestyle *Possessions held for enjoyment*			
Total net worth			

Getting a Grip on Your Expenses

It's hard to plan your cash flow for next month or for the next thirty years if you don't know your expenditures. I am still surprised how often potential new clients don't know what their retirement income need will be to cover expenses. Perhaps that's one of several reasons they seek our help. They hear about rules of thumb, such as "60 percent or 70 percent of preretirement income." Can you take a 30 percent pay cut the day you retire? Probably not, and it would not be much of a fun retirement, especially during the Active Phase.

Well, here's my rule of thumb, especially for the Active Phase: your retirement income need is very similar to what you spend today. Of course, there are some adjustments, which I will discuss in the next chapter.

The Confident Retirement Journey Approach™ to Looking at Your Expenses

To get a grip on your expenses and to possibly find "new" money that can make your retirement a solid reality, you need to track your expenses for a year to find your line-item totals. Chances are you already do that to some extent with an expense-tracking program, but here's how to organize your expenses using The Confident Retirement Journey Approach™. Break them down into three major categories:

1. Committed expenditures (includes ongoing and fixed obligations)
2. Somewhat discretionary expenditures
3. Very discretionary expenditures

The purpose of this exercise is to learn your *core* cost of living, thus making it easier to design realistic retirement projections. This can give you an edge on reaching retirement earlier or sustaining it longer because you can truly weigh your retirement priorities (such as when and how much to save for it) against lifestyle choices. Some of those lifestyle choices may be worth another year or two of work, or maybe not. It can also be a useful "lifeboat" drill in the event of a major financial setback, such as a layoff or another systemic financial crisis like we experienced in 2008–2010 (and longer for some people).

Important: If you have lifestyle assets, you should assign their maintenance or carrying costs in either the "somewhat discretionary expenditures" or "very discretionary expenditures" categories. For example, a time-share is clearly a lifestyle asset, and its monthly maintenance fees should reflect this because if you sold the time-share, you would have an increase in cash flow. The same could be said for the maintenance and insurance costs for that third or fourth vehicle in the driveway.

We all love our lifestyles and toys. Lifestyle assets or expenditures in and of themselves aren't bad—in fact, many of them are beneficial in terms of our well-being and satisfaction with life. A major purpose of retirement planning should be to find a good balance between the lifestyle assets you enjoy owning and the Financial Independence Assets that can provide you with retirement income. It takes both kinds to create a satisfying retirement—and a satisfying life before retirement. Looking at things in this way gives you a powerful tool to take control and set priorities.

Worksheet 3.2 The Confident Retirement Journey Expense Analysis™

Type	Monthly	Annual
Committed expenditures: ongoing *Food, clothing, utilities, insurance, medical, etc.*		
Committed expenditures: fixed *Debt service, taxes, college tuition, care for a dependent child or parent, etc.*		
Subtotal		
Somewhat discretionary expenditures *Basic entertainment, contributions, hobbies, gifts, organizations, etc.*		

Worksheet 3.2 (*continued*)

Very discretionary expenditures
  *Nice, but not necessary, home
  improvements, high-end entertainment,
  autos, art, boats, personal property,
  "toys," financial gifts to adult children,
  extended trips, etc.*		

Total		

Reviewing these totals, what do you think is practical to decrease if you had to cut back? What would be ideal if you didn't need to cut back? Does this seem like a budget to you? It shouldn't, as you are merely documenting where you are today and what your expenditures might look like during retirement. I'm a firm believer that diets and budgets don't work. At least they never have for me. Both of them seem to imply restraint, limits, and "can't-do attitudes." Nobody likes to be told, "You can't have that!" or "You can't do that!" So, I am proud to say that in over thirty-two years of counseling clients, I have never helped them develop a budget.

What, you say? You're a financial planner and you don't do budgets? Yes, that's right. It's not my business to tell people how to spend their money. But I have helped them do something better: set priorities. Without priorities, your immediate wants become too compelling and urgent. So instead of the "can't have" or "can't do" of a budget, why not let your important priorities do the heavy lifting for you? A vision of your child graduating from college can overpower an impulse purchase, so can the trip of a lifetime. Likewise, many people find that a vision of themselves in a trim new wardrobe can offset the urge for a second helping of chocolate cake.

Getting a Grip on Your Potential Unknowns

Contingent Assets and Obligations

Now you have a better idea of how you spend your money and the assets available to help you maintain a similar lifestyle during your retirement journey. But before we can see how these pieces fit together, there are some other important things to consider as you plan your journey. These may be unknowable right now, but you should give them some thought. They include a potential inheritance, the likelihood of continued employment, care for a dependent, and other things I discuss in more detail in chapter 7. I call these contingent assets and obligations, and they can be modeled and stated as a present or future value. Because they are unique to your situation, I won't generalize about them here.

Current Health and Probable Life Expectancy

Think about your retirement planning in terms of packing for a camping trip. A weekend jaunt is much easier to prepare for than a two-week backpacking trip into the wilderness. You don't need much for the short trip, and hey, if you run low on chocolate bars, you'll be back in a day. But how much should you pack for the long one? It's going to take more provisions and forethought, and so will a lengthy retirement.

We looked at some potential life expectancies in chapter 1, but those are probabilities using large populations. What really counts is *your* life expectancy. No one knows for certain, but these factors may narrow it down:

1. At what age did your parents, aunts, and uncles die? From what causes?
2. If they are still alive, how old are they, and how is their health? What are their major ailments (besides aches and pains)?
3. How is your health now? (Remember, all progress begins by telling the truth.) Perhaps you are taking much better care of

yourself than your parents did, so you need to factor that in. You might want to check out something like RealAge (www.realage.com) to help you estimate your life expectancy. This free online test analyzes your family health history, your health, and your lifestyle to give you an estimate of your actual age vs. your chronological age. (The results can be very joyful or depressing.)

You don't want to run out of money before you run out of life. So, pick a likely age and add *at least* another five years to it for good measure, perhaps ten years. Remember, life expectancy is also about your spouse or partner, if you have one. It's the life expectancy of the one likely to live the longest that counts. This estimate will help you in the next chapter as we look at what it will take to keep you on the road. You don't want to run out of gas before you get to your final destination.

Your Road Map Action Items

1. Complete The Confident Retirement Journey Balance Sheet™ (worksheet 3.1).
2. What is the amount of your Financial Independence Assets? _____.
3. Complete The Confident Retirement Journey Expense Analysis™ (worksheet 3.2). Based on the three categories of expenditures, what do you think is a reasonable estimate of your retirement expenditures per month?_____. Per year?_____.
4. What are your contingent obligations or assets, if any? _____.
5. What is your life-expectancy target? _____.

What's Your Number?

You can be young without money,
but you can't be old without it.
—Tennessee Williams

Okay, so you know approximately how much you spend today, how much of an asset base you have to support future spending, and approximately how long you may live. But how do you define *financial independence*? There are many ways to do it, mostly qualitative words like the ones I used to open chapter 2. They are good, but they need to be backed up by a measurable goal. You can't be confident about your retirement journey unless you know from the start what it will take to get you there. As I hinted in the last chapter, "there" is a difficult destination to find on a map—all you can do is estimate the length of your journey and what you think it will take in resources to get you there.

It's time to estimate your "number." I define this as a dollar amount of your Financial Independence Assets, as described in chapter 3. Once you have achieved this target, you can retire. Or, if you have already retired, you can sleep better.

Without knowing your number, three things may happen:

1. You keep working out of fear that you won't have enough, never realizing that maybe you already do.

2. You are unwilling to spend money and enjoy the fruits of your labor.

3. You take unnecessary risks with your money or invest too conservatively because you don't know how much you need.

Not knowing your number is like taking a very long vacation without credit cards; you don't know if you will have enough gas money for fun excursions or detours along the way. So, how do you go about finding it?

Finding Your Number

The 4 Percent Solution: Very Simple, but Not So Accurate

I alluded to the easiest method early in chapter 3 with my "back-of-the-napkin" calculations, which assumed a generous distribution rate of 5 percent. To determine a "safe withdrawal rate," or the amount you can take from your portfolio without depleting it, *simply subtract your estimated annual Social Security and pension benefits from the annual income you want at retirement, and then divide that by 0.04.* For example, if you need $100,000 after annual Social Security and pension benefits, then you would need $2.5 million. This assumes that you know what your inflation-adjusted income need is at the start of retirement and that your $2.5 million produces a 4 percent return that you can spend every year. If it does, and you don't experience any inflation, then your kids or your favorite charities get a nice bequest. The odds are, however, that you will experience inflation and unexpected expenses, so you may not have much left over at the end of a thirty-year retirement.

Why divide by 4 percent? You could divide by 5 percent, like I did in chapter 3, or divide by 3 percent to be more conservative. However, over the past eighteen years, numerous academic papers have been written about the safe withdrawal rate, the first and most famous one being William Bengen's 1994 award-winning paper in the *Journal of Financial Planning.*[16] Using historical data back to 1926, he constructed rolling thirty-year periods with portfolios that included at least 50 percent stocks. His conclusion? You could safely withdraw 4.15 percent of what your portfolio was worth when you started retirement, and you could adjust that amount each year for inflation. Many periods—including those near a market bottom—had even higher starting withdrawal rates, but the average was 4.15 percent. And portfolios with less than 50 percent stocks had a safe withdrawal rate as low as 2.5 percent.

Other studies, such as the Trinity Study in 1998, came up with similar results.[17] Researchers took various portfolio mixes, such as 50 percent stocks and 50 percent bonds and analyzed how they would have done at different withdrawal rates adjusted for inflation over the past eighty-plus years. Most of the subsequent studies, including a very recent one with 140 years of data,[18] basically confirm this number, assuming that the retiree makes adjustments along the way as their age, health, portfolio value, bond yields, etc. change.

But please don't take this 4 percent as gospel. In any of these studies, *when* one retired made a huge difference. Those who retired at a market bottom obviously did much better than those who may have started near the top in, say, 1928 or 2000. The unlucky ones took withdrawals in a down market, making it very difficult for their portfolios to recover. And these studies don't mean that it is safe to withdraw 4 percent of the market value every year, *they mean 4 percent of the value at the start of retirement.* This means you could be taking out more than 4 percent during bad years and less than 4 percent during good years to meet that inflation-adjusted amount you started with at the beginning of retirement. You will need the good years of portfolio growth to replenish the bad ones.

Once again, these studies included equities (stocks) in the portfolio. The 4 percent rule of thumb will not work with portfolios heavy in bonds, certificates of deposits (CDs), and Treasury bills. You would need to use a lower estimate of 2.5 percent, perhaps lower now in 2013, given where we are in the interest-rate cycle.

If you are already retired and don't have time to accumulate your number, another way to use this formula is to take your Financial Independence Assets from The Confident Retirement Journey Balance Sheet™ (worksheet 3.1) in chapter 3 and divide by 0.04. This will give you a degree of confidence about what you can spend without seriously depleting your portfolio over the years of good, average, or bad returns. Many of our clients take more, but we monitor it every year and make adjustments. We may start out with a lower withdrawal percentage at the beginning of retirement, and then open up the wallet with a higher withdrawal rate as clients age and as conditions warrant.

Nine Steps for a More Accurate Result

The 4 percent solution is a quick and easy one. But we're talking about *your* retirement here, so it rightfully deserves a more accurate answer (short of consulting with a financial advisor with robust software that isn't provided by a brokerage firm, mutual fund, or insurance company).

The following six key drivers will help you better estimate how much in Financial Independence Assets you need for what I call your Financial Independence Number, or your number for short:

1. Retirement lifestyle expenses
2. Years to retirement
3. Inflation
4. Social Security and pension income
5. Longevity
6. After-tax investment returns

(You may want to glance at worksheets 4.1 and 4.2 in this chapter to get an overview of how all these drivers come together, and then return back here to Driver 1 to begin.)

DRIVER 1
Retirement Lifestyle Expenses

STEP 1: Calculate your retirement lifestyle expenses.

To know your number, you first need to define your retirement lifestyle in terms of dollars. In the last chapter, you calculated your current expense estimate using The Confident Retirement Journey Expense Analysis™ (worksheet 3.2). With a little thought, it takes a few adjustments to arrive at an estimate of your retirement lifestyle expenses. Your objective is to get a handle on what your monthly retirement lifestyle expenses might be, which may be similar to what you spend now but may have some key differences.

Here are the steps to identify the differences in your expenditures now and in retirement. A summary is in worksheet 4.1.

STEP 1A: WRITE DOWN THE CURRENT EXPENSE ESTIMATE FROM THE
CONFIDENT RETIREMENT JOURNEY EXPENSE ANALYSIS™
(WORKSHEET 3.2).

	Monthly	Annual
Current expense estimate	$	$

STEP 1B: REVIEW THE ONGOING COMMITTED EXPENDITURES
CATEGORY IN THE CONFIDENT RETIREMENT JOURNEY
EXPENSES ANALYSIS™ AND IDENTIFY ANY HEALTH
INSURANCE COSTS THAT MIGHT CHANGE IN RETIREMENT.

Is your employer paying in part or full for any health care costs on a pretax basis? If so, you need to make sure that they are included in your estimate of retirement expenditures. Even though you will have Medicare starting at age sixty-five, you will want to purchase a supplement to it. Medicare covers about 80 percent of typical medical costs,[19] so you'll need to pick up the other 20 percent. This isn't a big deal in the early years, but it can be as your health deteriorates.

Meanwhile, Medicare costs are means-tested; the premiums can go up to more than $300 a month for people in the higher tax brackets, and today those wealthier clients are also paying more for Part D coverage. Medigap coverage can reduce some of the risk of catastrophic co-pays, but of course, that comes at a cost, too. And what about employer-paid disability or life insurance? You may not need those in retirement, so these expenses can be dropped from your estimate. However, you should consider adding in long-term care insurance, which I recommend for about 80 percent of my retirement planning clients.

Calculating step 1B: Health insurance adjustment

	Monthly	Annual
Employer-paid health insurance premium (if retiring before age 65)	$	$
Medicare supplement policy	+	+
Long-term care policy	+	+
Disability policy	–	–
Step 1B total: Health insurance adjustment	=	=

STEP 1C: IDENTIFY ANY EMPLOYER-PAID FRINGE BENEFITS YOU ARE CURRENTLY RECEIVING.

Do you have a company vehicle or an expense account? You may need to pay those expenses on your own dime. I know this hits a lot of small business owners who do a good job of keeping their income taxes down during their working years with company-owned autos, entertainment expenses, and so on. They suddenly experience a spike in personal expenditures upon retirement.

Calculating step 1C: Employer-paid fringe benefits adjustment

	Monthly	Annual
Employer-paid vehicle expenses	$	$

Employer-paid expenses (phones, computers, etc.)	+	+
Other employer-paid lifestyle expenses	+	+
Step 1C total: Employer-paid fringe benefits adjustment	=	=

STEP 1D: REVIEW THE FIXED COMMITTED EXPENDITURES CATEGORY IN THE CONFIDENT RETIREMENT JOURNEY EXPENSE ANALYSIS™ (WORKSHEET 3.2) AND IDENTIFY ITEMS THAT WILL LIKELY DISAPPEAR BY THE START OF YOUR PROJECTED RETIREMENT DATE.

For many people that would be mortgage payments, college tuition bills, and perhaps other expenses related to raising children. NOTE: If they will be gone within a couple of years after you retire, go ahead and subtract them. If they are going to be present for a while, leave them in. We are trying to arrive at a number that will give you the confidence to retire, so it is better to err on the side of higher expenditures during retirement.

Calculating step 1D: Fixed committed expenditures likely to disappear

	Monthly	Annual
Mortgage payments	$	$
Child expenses (including health and auto insurance, phone bills, etc.)	+	+
Tuition and other college expenses	+	+
Other	+	+
Step 1D total: Fixed committed expenditures likely to disappear	=	=

STEP 1E: MAKE ADDITIONAL ADJUSTMENTS FOR TRAVEL, VEHICLES, MAJOR EXPENDITURES, ETC.

Big vacations, major home repairs, or periodic new vehicle purchases take a bite out of your savings and distort your true living costs over a longer time period. "Well, that was just a one-time expense," you might say. But as the saying goes, "It's always something." Retirement is for the rest of your life, not the rest of the year.

Some things like clothing and commuting costs are less, and hopefully the kids are launched and the mortgage is paid off. But these are more than offset by travel, time for hobbies, and other things. This is especially true in the early Active Phase of retirement. As retirees age, the spending gradually decreases until medical expenses start kicking in, and along the way, vehicles and roofs usually need replacing. Financial planners with sophisticated software can model these special costs into retirement projections for you, but for now it's important to get a rough estimate.

Table 4.1 Expenses during retirement*

Typically higher	Typically lower
Vacation	Home furnishings
Hobbies	College education
Gifts	Weddings
Entertainment	Business wardrobes
Home maintenance	Personal-care items
Uncovered medical expenses	Transportation/commuting

*As the fine print always says, "Your results may vary."

If you plan to buy a new car every ten years, I suggest taking today's price of it, dividing that amount by 120 (ten years times twelve months per year), and adding that to your annual retirement lifestyle expense number. Likewise, if you want to take a $6,000 vacation every year, you would add $500 to your monthly lifestyle expenditure amount. And what about all those pesky unexpected things like hot water heaters, repairs, etc.? It might be wise to add another amount to your monthly total. These three things aren't expenditures every month but rather an amount that goes into an earmarked side fund to be used when the need arises.

Calculating step 1E: Travel, vehicles, major expenditures, etc. adjustment

	Monthly	Annual
Travel, vehicles, repairs, and other major expenses	$	$

Now, put it all together in worksheet 4.1 to find your estimated retirement lifestyle expenses.

Worksheet 4.1 Calculating your retirement lifestyle expenses

Steps	Monthly	Annual
1A. Current expense estimate (from worksheet 3.2)	$	$
1B. Health insurance adjustment	+	+
1C. Employer-paid fringe benefits adjustment	+	+
1D. Fixed committed expenditures likely to disappear	−	−
1E: Travel, vehicles, major expenditures, etc. adjustment	+	+
Step 1 total: Retirement lifestyle expense estimate	=	=

© 2013 Ron Kelemen. PDF form available at www.ConfidentRetirementJourney.com.

Congratulations! You now have completed step 1 of finding your number by estimating your retirement lifestyle expenses. Now that you have it, the next steps are easier.

Years to Retirement

When you retire makes a big difference, both good and bad. The longer the time between now and when you retire, the more time you have to save money and accrue pension and Social Security benefits—

while at the same time giving your investments time to grow. The flip side, however, is that inflation increases the amount of the retirement lifestyle expenses you just calculated on worksheet 4.1. You can see in table 4.2 later in this chapter how the cost per $1,000 of retirement expenses increases with time at various inflation rates, and that leads us to the next driver of your Financial Independence Number.

STEP 2: Select your estimated years to retirement.

Years to retirement	

Inflation

At 4 percent, prices double approximately every eighteen years, based on our old "friend" the Rule of 72 (covered in chapter 1). Remember, you could easily be retired for thirty or forty-five years, perhaps longer than you worked. Thus, $1 million of Financial Independence Assets in 2013 with 4 percent inflation would be the equivalent of only $500,000 in the year 2030. What costs $1 today would cost $2 at that time. Imagine—how old will you be then?

STEP 3: Select an inflation assumption.

I'd suggest starting at 4 percent, because it is close to the rate for the past fifty years and more likely to cover some of the expenses of retirees that are not accurately tracked by the CPI. You can always choose a higher number or a lower one like 3 percent, which is close to the long-term average all the way back to 1926. For my examples, however, I will use 4 percent.

Inflation assumption	%

STEP 4: Estimate your inflation-adjusted retirement lifestyle expenses.

Let's say, for example, on worksheet 4.1 you think your retirement lifestyle expenses will be about $8,000 per month on average, taking into account trips, occasional vehicle and roof replacements, etc. You will need to inflate that by your guess of the inflation rate.

To do this, consult table 4.2 and find the amount in the table that most closely matches your years to retirement and your inflation estimate. Then, take your monthly retirement lifestyle expenses (from worksheet 4.1) and multiply this number by the figure from table 4.2. That is the amount it will take to produce the same spending power per $1,000 of monthly income desired.

Table 4.2 Inflation adjustment for retirement costs at start of retirement (per $1,000 of costs today)

Years to retirement	Inflation rates					
	2%	3%	4%	5%	6%	7%
3	1.061	1.093	1.125	1.158	1.191	1.225
5	1.104	1.159	1.217	1.276	1.338	1.402
7	1.149	1.230	1.316	1.407	1.504	1.606
10	1.219	1.344	1.480	1.629	1.791	1.967
12	1.268	1.426	1.601	1.886	2.012	2.252
15	1.346	1.558	1.801	2.079	2.396	2.759
20	1.486	1.806	2.191	2.653	3.207	3.869
25	1.641	2.094	2.665	3.386	4.292	5.427
30	1.811	2.427	3.243	4.322	5.743	7.612

Using my example, if you think you will need $8,000 per month ten years from now, multiply 1.480 by $8,000. That amounts to $11,840 per month ten years from now to have the same purchasing power you enjoy today at $8,000. That's over $142,000 per year! If you're one year away, no big deal. But if you're ten, fifteen, or twenty-five years away, those are scary numbers. And the number gets much bigger as you go through retirement. If you are already retired, this gives you an idea of what your monthly costs would be in the future. If you're seventy and already living on $8,000 per month, by age eighty you'll need about $3,840 more per month at 4 percent inflation, assuming your lifestyle and medical expenses don't change.

Calculating step 4: Your inflation-adjusted retirement lifestyle expenses

	Monthly	Annual
Retirement lifestyle expense (from worksheet 4.1)	$	$
Inflation adjustment (using table 4.2)	x	x
Inflation-adjusted retirement lifestyle expenses total	=	=

DRIVER 4

Social Security and Pension Income

So far, we've been focusing only upon your expenditures. It's time to factor in some resources that will help lower the amount of money you will need from your Financial Independence Assets every year. The two key resources here are Social Security and pension income. The nice thing about Social Security is that it has a cost-of-living adjustment (COLA) most years, but whether it will keep up with inflation remains to be seen. It is, however, better than pension plans (like my late father's) that don't include COLAs. Although many public employee pension plans also have COLAs, private employer pensions generally do not, and they are becoming increasingly rare as companies switch to defined contribution plans such as 401(k)s. If you have a private employer plan without a COLA, you may want to assume a higher rate of inflation, which will increase the size of your number, or you may want to consult with a financial planner who can model several different cash flows more accurately than the do-it-yourself method I'm describing here.

Social Security's very user-friendly website at www.socialsecurity .gov has excellent calculators, including one that utilizes your own work history and your projected age of retirement. Some public and private employer pension plans have websites to help you estimate your projected benefit; others have a formula to apply that takes into account your years of service and final pay. Unfortunately, the Social Security calculators do not factor inflation increases. The number you see at, say, sixty-six is what you would get if there were no inflation adjustments, so you need to factor that in—especially if you are several years from retirement.

STEP 5: Estimate your inflation-adjusted Social Security and pension income.

As in step 4, the easiest way to do this is to use table 4.2. Take the Social Security estimate and multiply by the number in table 4.2. For example, if Social Security estimates your benefit to be $2,300 at age sixty-six, you are ten years from retirement, and you assume 4 percent inflation, then you would multiply $2,300 by 1.480 to arrive at $3,404 per month. If you want to be more conservative, then take a lower COLA assumption, such as 2 percent. Then add in your pension income, if you will have one.

Calculating step 5: Your inflation-adjusted Social Security and pension income

	Monthly	Annual
Social Security estimate	$	$
Inflation adjustment (using table 4.2)	x	x
Pension estimate	+	+
Inflation-adjusted Social Security and pension income total	=	=

STEP 6: Subtract your monthly inflation-adjusted Social Security and pension income from your monthly inflation-adjusted retirement lifestyle expense estimate.

	Monthly	Annual
Inflation-adjusted retirement lifestyle expenses (from step 4)	$	$
Inflation-adjusted Social Security and pension income (from step 5)	−	−
Financial Independence Assets need total	=	=

In my example, this would be $11,840 minus $3,404, which would be $8,436 monthly and $101,232 annually. This is the annual amount of income that will need to be supported by your Financial Independence Assets.

DRIVER 5

Longevity

Remember our discussion on longevity? Use the age you noted at the end of chapter 3. What we are trying to do here is arrive at the length of your retirement. So, say you want to retire at age sixty-five, and you think you will live to ninety-five. That means thirty years of retirement.

STEP 7: Select your longevity, or estimated length of retirement.

Estimated years of retirement	

After-Tax Investment Returns

STEP 8: Select a likely long-term after-tax investment return.

Next, you'll need to target an after-tax rate of return on your investments. I'll get into how you arrive at that number and how you might need to invest to get there in the next chapter. But for now, let's assume a reasonable *after-tax* rate of return on your Financial Independence Assets of 5 percent.

Estimated after-tax investment return	%

STEP 9: Put it all together to find your Financial Independence Number.

Consult table 4.3, 4.4, or 4.5, depending upon the assumed rate of inflation in Driver 3. I'll use table 4.4 as an example because it assumes a 4 percent inflation rate.

In table 4.4, find where the 5 percent After-Tax Rate of Return column intersects with the 30 in the Years of Retirement row, and then brace yourself. It will take almost $25,000 to produce $1,000 of income per year at 4 percent inflation at an assumed 5 percent after-tax rate of return for 30 years. Doing the math in worksheet 4.2, it will take over $2.5 million at the start of your retirement to provide you with $101,232 annually or $8,436 of inflation-adjusted income per month. "What!" You say? "That's outrageous!" Yes, it is, especially since so few Americans spending over $8,000 per month have just a fraction of that in Financial Independence Assets right now.

Table 4.3 Assets required to produce $1,ooo per year at 3% inflation

Years of retirement	After-tax rate of return							
	1%	2%	3%	4%	5%	6%	7%	8%
45	$70,832	$55,120	$43,689	$35,260	$28,956	$24,176	$20,499	$17,631
40	59,548	47,735	38,835	32,055	26,832	22,762	19,554	16,997
35	49,317	40,701	33,981	28,692	24,494	21,130	18,411	16,194
30	40,042	34,002	29,126	25,163	21,919	19,246	17,028	15,176
25	31,633	27,622	24,272	21,459	19,085	17,072	15,356	13,885
20	24,009	21,546	19,417	17,571	15,965	14,562	13,332	12,250
15	17,098	15,759	14,563	13,492	12,530	11,664	10,883	10,177
10	10,831	10,248	9,709	9,210	8,748	8,319	7,921	7,550
5	5,150	4,999	4,854	4,716	4,584	4,457	4,336	4,220

Table 4.4 Assets required to produce $1,000 per year at 4% inflation

Years of retirement	After-tax rate of return							
	1%	2%	3%	4%	5%	6%	7%	8%
45	$91,094	$69,802	$54,463	$43,269	$34,990	$28,782	$24,063	$20,425
40	74,154	58,717	47,179	38,462	31,804	26,662	22,646	19,475
35	59,520	48,658	40,237	33,654	28,461	24,330	21,013	18,328
30	46,878	39,529	33,624	28,846	24,955	21,765	19,131	16,942
25	35,958	31,245	27,322	24,038	21,277	18,943	16,961	15,269
20	26,524	23,728	21,317	19,231	17,419	15,840	14,459	13,247
15	18,375	16,906	15,596	14,423	13,372	12,426	11,575	10,807
10	11,335	10,716	10,144	9,615	9,126	8,672	8,251	7,859
5	5,253	5,098	4,950	4,808	4,672	4,542	4,418	4,299

Table 4.5 Assets required to produce $1,000 per year at 5% inflation

Years of Retirement	After-tax rate of return							
	1%	2%	3%	4%	5%	6%	7%	8%
45	$118,548	$89,521	$68,799	$53,822	$42,857	$34,724	$28,610	$23,951
40	93,211	72,945	57,908	46,635	38,095	31,556	26,493	22,531
35	72,346	58,605	48,015	39,784	33,333	28,234	24,168	20,898
30	55,164	46,201	39,029	33,254	28,571	24,751	21,612	19,017
25	41,014	35,470	30,867	27,028	23,810	21,098	18,803	16,851
20	29,362	26,186	23,453	21,093	19,048	17,269	15,717	14,358
15	19,767	18,156	16,719	15,436	14,286	13,254	12,325	11,488
10	11,865	11,209	10,603	10,042	9,524	9,043	8,598	8,184
5	5,358	5,199	5,047	4,901	4,762	4,629	4,501	4,379

Worksheet 4.2 Finding your Financial Independence Number

Steps	Per example	Your number
1. Write your retirement lifestyle expenses estimate (Driver 1, total from worksheet 4.1).	$8,000	
2. Select your years to retirement (Driver 2).	10 years	
3. Select an inflation assumption (Driver 3).	4%	
4. Estimate your inflation-adjusted retirement lifestyle expenses using table 4.2 (Driver 3).	$11,840	
5. Estimate your inflation-adjusted Social Security income, using table 4.2. Add pension income, if you will have one (Driver 4).	$3,404	
6. Subtract your monthly inflation-adjusted Social Security and pension income (Driver 4, step 5) from your monthly inflation-adjusted retirement lifestyle expense estimate (Driver 3, step 4) to arrive at your Financial Independence Assets need. Multiply by 12 to get your annual need.	$11,840-$3,404= $8,436 x 12 = $101,232	
7. Select your length of retirement (Driver 5).	30	
8. Select an after-tax investment return (Driver 6).	5%	
9. Use table 4.3, 4.4, or 4.5 to find the assets required to produce $1,000 per year. Then find the thousands number of your annual Financial Independence Assets need (Driver 4, step 6) by moving the decimal three points to the left. Multiply these numbers together.	$24,955 x 101.232= $2,526,244	
YOUR FINANCIAL INDEPENDENCE NUMBER	$2.53 MILLION	

© 2013 Ron Kelemen. PDF form available at www.ConfidentRetirementJourney.com.

Don't believe these numbers? Let's do a little reverse engineering. Multiply that $2.5 million by 0.05. That would produce an annual income of $125,000 per year, which is more than the $101,000 you needed. However, in six years with 4 percent inflation, you will need $125,000 to buy what $101,000 buys now. What happens from years seven through thirty? You must consume principal to stay even with inflation. So much for leaving an inheritance.

I will be the first to admit that this is a simplistic way of finding your number, but it's something you can do right here on these pages without the aid of complicated software and spreadsheets. You most likely used different assumptions and came up with a different number for your projected retirement lifestyle expenses. Changes to any one of the drivers can change your estimated Financial Independence Number. This process uses straight-line assumptions, and we all know that any journey has curves in the road and different speeds along the way. So, take the results with a few grains of salt.

Finding Your Number: Going Beyond Static Investment Assumptions

If you want a more accurate forecast of your number with changing assumptions (like a mortgage payoff in year ten, no COLA with a private pension plan, changing investment returns, part-time work, no travel budget after age seventy-five, etc.), you may need to enlist the services of a financial advisor who isn't trying to sell you something. Even then, the one guarantee I make to my clients is that their results will never come out exactly as projected. The variability of investment returns is the main reason. Let's roll the dice to see why.

Imagine that you rolled a 5 six times in a row, as shown in example 1. The odds of that are way below 1 percent, and the odds of replicating six years in a row of 5 percent returns are also very slim. But if you did, at the end of six years, you would have withdrawn $50,000 each year and still had your $1 million left.

Example 1 The perfect world

Year	1	2	3	4	5	6
Return	5%	5%	5%	5%	5%	5%
Net year-end value	$1,000,000	$1,000,000	$1,000,000	$1,000,000	$1,000,000	$1,000,000

$1,000,000 portfolio; $50,000 withdrawn at end of each year; 5% avg. return years 1–6

Now, example 2 shows you weren't so lucky—it wasn't quite a perfect world. Your retirement started off badly, but your portfolio rallied nicely in the last two years. However, even though you averaged a 5 percent return, your ending balance was worth a lot less.

 Example 2 The not-so-perfect world

Year	1	2	3	4	5	6
Return	-20%	-5%	0%	+5%	20%	30%
Net year-end value	$750,000	$662,500	$612,500	$593,125	$661,750	$810,275

$1,000,000 portfolio; $50,000 withdrawn at end of each year; 5% avg. return years 1–6

And in the not-so-perfect-but-better world of example 3, you also averaged a 5 percent return. Here you started off strong but fizzled in the end. However, because you started out well, your portfolio balance was pretty close to where it started six years earlier.

 Example 3 The not-so-perfect-but-better world

Year	1	2	3	4	5	6
Return	+30%	+20%	+5%	0%	5%	-20%
Net year-end value	$1,250,000	$1,450,000	$1,472,500	$1,422,500	$1,301,375	$991,100

$1,000,000 portfolio; $50,000 withdrawn at end of each year; 5% avg. return years 1–6

So you had three different possibilities, all averaging 5 percent per year. If you've ever fly-fished, you know that it is possible to drown even when a river's average depth is only one foot. It's those pesky deep holes that can fill the waders!

Figure 4.1 Three different possibilities averaging 5%

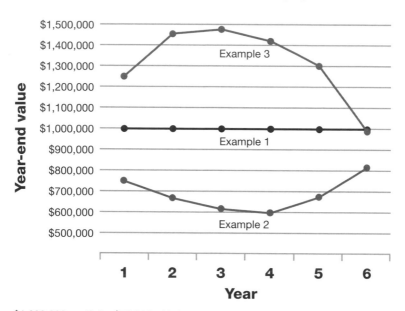

$1,000,000 portfolio; $50,000 withdrawn at end of each year; 5% avg. return years 1–6

These were only three hypothetical scenarios over six periods. Now imagine many possibilities and sequences over a thirty- or forty-year retirement. Your results might look something like figure 4.2, which is quite different from the assumed straight-line projection.

How can you plan a retirement with so many possible outcomes? Many financial advisors are now using Monte Carlo software to back up their projections. I know—Monte Carlo and retirement planning shouldn't be used in the same sentence unless you are extremely wealthy. But in this case, it means running thousands of scenarios with varying rates of return to get a probability of "success" (success being defined as having your money outlive you). This probability is like a weather forecast: if you have a high probability of sunshine, you go to the beach. If not, you make other plans.

Figure 4.2 The variability of results

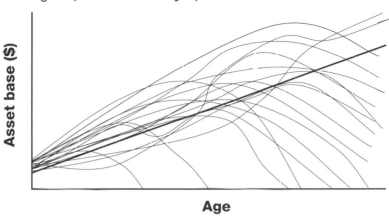

Monte Carlo simulations can be misused, their assumptions need careful tuning, and they have limitations that I won't go into here, but they are better than assuming straight-line forecasts. If, however, you would rather keep it simple and use the formula we walked through in this chapter, lower your assumed rate of return or your spending needs, both of which could change your number.

Whether you feel reasonably confident about where you are today or feel totally overwhelmed by the size of the number, you now have a starting point and a target. In the next chapter, we will explore how you can either revise your number downward or get to it by the time you retire.

Your Road Map Action Items

1. Find your latest Social Security estimate or get it online at www.socialsecurity.gov. _____.
2. Complete worksheets 4.1 and 4.2.
3. What is your number? _____.
4. What do you think about it?
5. How could you change your expenses to lower it?

Ron Kelemen

How Do You Get There?

Compound interest is the eighth wonder of the universe.
—Albert Einstein*

*One of many quotes attributed to him long after
he died, but it turns out he never said it.

Okay, so now you have an approximate number. You may be energized just knowing what it is. You might already be there, close to it, or you know that you need to get to work. You might be scared or discouraged. If so, this book is for you, especially this chapter. Let's first get an overview of six basic options, and then I will go over some in more detail.

Option 1: Hope for the Best

Maybe you'll get lucky with a lottery ticket or an inheritance. Or maybe inflation will be lower than the 4 percent we assumed. Or maybe we're on the verge of increasing interest rates or a major and long-lasting bull market. But as a strategy, hope alone won't build your confidence at the start of your retirement journey. So yes, by all means, hope—but plan for the worst, or at least the not so good.

Option 2: Work Longer, Possibly Part-Time during Retirement

If you were planning to retire at a relatively young age, *delaying retirement* is the single best thing you can do to make your retirement more secure. Why do I say this? Over the years, my team and I have run many retirement-feasibility scenarios for clients. We've seen firsthand the difference one or more years of continued work can make—far more than the rate of return on your investments—especially as you get older. Every year that you work is a year you are building pension and Social Security credits and adding to your 401(k). Above all, you are not taking withdrawals from your Financial Independence Assets.

Let's say you are just turning sixty-two and considering retiring with $1 million of Financial Independence Assets that earn an assumed 7 percent, and you need to withdraw $40,000 per year. By the time you are sixty-six and at full retirement age (for most of today's baby boomers), your assets will have drained down to $871,000, and at 7 percent, they will never get back to your $1 million starting point. In fact, your financial assets will have been completely depleted in just over twenty-four years, and you will have locked yourself into at least a 25 percent "pay cut" from Social Security—much more if COLAs were considered. If your full retirement age is sixty-seven, you will have locked in at least a 30 percent reduction in benefits for life.

Meanwhile, had you kept working and not touched the $1 million, your Financial Independence Assets would have grown to $1,225,043. (To equal the same result if you had retired at age sixty-two, your assets would have needed to earn 8.88 percent—and much more than that if you had continued to add to your nest egg before starting withdrawals at age sixty-six.) Furthermore, your Social Security benefit would be at least 25 percent higher had you waited. Finally, working longer usually gives you the cash-flow ability to keep saving, so the $1,225,043 would be even higher if you had continued to save from age sixty-two to sixty-six.

While working longer is good if you can do so, don't bet your retirement security on working into your late sixties or seventies. For some, that may not be possible. Some people have the type of job where they can dial it back a little by working part-time. Other jobs are more of an all-or-nothing affair, and some jobs are physically demanding. Even if working longer or phasing out gradually is possible, you cannot be certain that you or your spouse will have the health to make it happen.

Some might argue that work is another asset class and an important part of the retirement-income portfolio. It is also fulfilling for many people. As Mitch Anthony, author of *The New Retirementality* defines it, "work is adding value to others while adding meaning to your life."[20] We have many clients who retire briefly, then return to work. Most don't do so for financial reasons but because of boredom, lack of social interactions, and the need for a sense of purpose. To the extent that working longer also brings in additional income, that's great.

Option 3: Save More in Your Working Years

This is something over which you have some control, particularly if you are not yet retired. I'll discuss that shortly.

Option 4: Reduce Your Retirement Lifestyle Expenditures

This lowers your Financial Independence Number. Besides working longer, this is the next-best thing you can do to create a sustainable investment. If you start practicing living on less now, you will be in a better position to work on option 3 above, which is saving more in your working years.

Option 5: Earn More on Your Financial Independence Assets

In this era of low interest rates, this is a hot topic for many people.

Like option 3 above, this is something over which you may have some control, but not always. It is closely connected to how much you need to save and how much you can spend during retirement. I'll have more about that later.

Option 6: Die Earlier

This is not really an option in most states. All joking aside, if your genetics, lifestyle, and state of health aren't favorable, perhaps you won't need to plan for an extended retirement. Your number could be lower.

Back to Option 3: Save More in Your Working Years

Quite often, my colleagues and I hear from relatively new clients, "Where were you when I was thirty?" or, "I wish I had started saving sooner," or, "You need to talk to my kids and get them started early." Why do they say this? They know it's all about compound interest, which is magnified exponentially by time.

Time and the rate of compounding are your most important allies in wealth accumulation when you are saving for retirement. They can also be your worst enemies during retirement, with inflation and longevity. Take a look at figure 5.1 and table 5.1.

As you can see in figure 5.1, not much happens at the assumed 3 percent return for a few years, and not much happens for the first five to ten years, regardless of your rate of return. Where things really take off is with the higher returns over time. Your rate of return really matters the further out you go in time.

The actual cost of procrastination is shown in table 5.1. Let's say you have twenty-five years before retirement, and you plan to save $100 per month with a target rate of 7 percent. Over the course of a year, that takes $3.29 per day, or the price of a latte. That means you would have $80,786 by the time you retire. But suppose you put it off for a year, leaving only twenty-four years of savings. You would

Figure 5.1 $100 per month at various rates of return

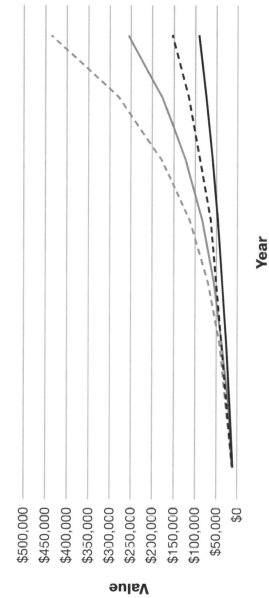

	5	10	15	20	25	30	35	40
3%	$6,522	$14,122	$22,934	$33,149	$44,990	$58,718	$74,633	$93,082
5%	6,889	15,755	27,070	41,511	59,943	83,466	113,488	151,805
7%	7,274	17,586	32,049	52,334	80,786	120,690	176,658	255,156
9%	7,676	19,638	38,043	66,362	109,934	176,976	280,127	438,838

Year

Value

1–40 years, compounded annually at 5-year increments

have only $74,301, a difference of $6,485. That difference, divided by 365 days in your year of procrastination, comes to a whopping $17.77 per day. To achieve the same results of investing a year earlier, you would need to save not just $100 per month but $108.60 for the next twenty-four years. These aren't your numbers? Simply divide all the numbers by half if all you can invest is $50 per month. Or multiply everything by ten if you can invest $1,000 per month.

Table 5.1 Cost of one year of procrastination at 7%

Years to retirement	Annual return $100 per month ($3.29 per day) compounded monthly	Annual cost	Daily cost	Additional cost per month to make up difference
14	$28,752	$3,297	$9.03	$12.83
15	$32,049			
19	47,711	4,624	12.67	10.35
20	52,334			
24	74,301	6,485	17.77	8.60
25	80,786			

The numbers are even greater for the thirty- to forty-year time periods and for greater rates of return and amounts saved, but I think you get the point: time matters.

You should now have a better understanding about the power of time and rate of return. As I said earlier, the amount you save in your accumulation years is also important.

Another way to get a better sense of what it will take to reach your number is shown in figure 5.2, which illustrates how much it takes per month to reach $1 million. If $1 million is half of what you need, double those numbers. If what you need is less than $1 million, say $500,000, simply cut those numbers in half.

Note the curve on this graph is the mirror image of figure 5.1. Even though it is shaped differently, it illustrates the importance of time

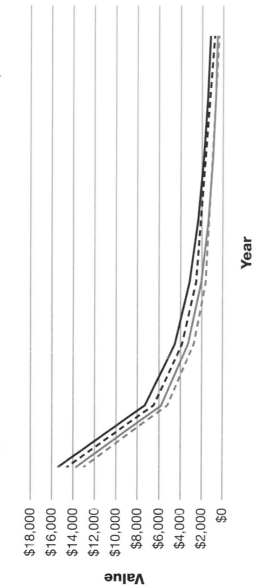

Figure 5.2 Monthly investment required to reach $1,000,000 at various rates of return

	5	10	15	20	25	30	35	40
—— 3%	$15,239	$7,057	$4,350	$3,011	$2,219	$1,701	$1,338	$1,073
– – 5%	14,363	6,310	3,678	2,400	1,663	1,195	879	657
—— 7%	13,543	5,637	3,099	1,900	1,231	824	563	390
– – 9%	12,775	5,032	2,604	1,494	903	561	354	226

1–40 years, compounded annually at 5-year increments

and rate of return. If you are fifteen years away from retirement, it will take $4,350 per month, or $52,200 per year, to reach $1 million. But if you invest more for growth, say 9 percent, it takes only $2,604 per month, or $31,248 annually.

If you are fortunate enough to be reading this in your late twenties or early thirties and you can afford to invest just a few hundred per month, it's much easier to accumulate large sums, especially if some of that amount is contributed by your employer in a 401(k) account. Now you know why some of our older clients wish they had met us sooner and why they want their young adult children to get investing early.

"But," you ask, "I'm fifty, and there is no way I can save that kind of money right now. What can I do?" That's why I wrote this book. All too often, we have had prospective clients come in the door, clueless about what it will take to retire comfortably. But you have an advantage. If you have gone through the exercises of determining your assets and expenditures as outlined in chapter 3 and have estimated your number in chapter 4, you are in much better shape than a majority of people who have done nothing.

So, to answer the "What can I do" question, go back to the beginning of this chapter. Options 2, 3, 4, and 5 are still within your control: work longer, save more in your working years, reduce your retirement lifestyle expenditures (which may help you with option 3), and earn more on your Financial Independence Assets. No single thing is going to help, but a combination of several most likely will. Can't save $1,000 more per month? Well, even $100 helps; working an extra year helps, if you have that opportunity; planning on a slightly reduced retirement lifestyle budget helps. Doing nothing is not an option.

Back to Option 5: Earn More on Your Financial Independence Assets

By now, you may have noticed that earning more on your money can make a big difference. Remember tables 4.3, 4.4, and 4.5 in chapter 4?

These showed that the higher your after-tax return, the lower your number. If you already have a lump sum of assets, you might want to peek ahead to table 8.2, which shows how much a lump sum grows at different rates of return over time. You may not have complete control over how long you will be able to work, and you might be on a very tight budget just to make ends meet. But you do have some degree of control over how much your Financial Independence Assets may potentially earn *over the long run*.

Your Road Map Action Items

1. Based on your retirement vision from chapter 2, your current job, and your health, is working longer an option?
2. Which of the six options are possible for you?
3. How much more can you save on a regular basis? _____.
4. Identify your lazy dollars that could be working harder for you.

Ron Kelemen

Putting Your Financial Independence Assets to Work

You don't need to be a rocket scientist. Investing is not a game where the guy with the 160 IQ beats the guy with 130 IQ.
—Warren Buffet

Risk: The Preface for Any Discussion about Investing

Some of the most anxious retirees and preretirees I know could improve their financial prospects simply by taking at least some of their Financial Independence Assets out from under the mattress. They are concerned with how stocks, bonds, or mutual funds fluctuate in value and affect their net worth in the short run; and at the same time, they are concerned about the adequacy of their Financial Independence Assets. I get it. I think everybody gets it, especially after what we went through from 2008 onward.

However, in this low-interest-rate environment, it is nearly impossible to keep up with inflation and taxes in traditional "safe" savings vehicles. If inflation is 3 percent, and you are earning 3 percent, what is your real (inflation-adjusted) return? *It's zero.* But wait—

don't forget about taxes. If you are in a combined 35 percent federal and state tax bracket, you first must pay taxes on the full 3 percent of earnings before inflation takes its toll, which leaves you with a net return of −1.05 percent after both inflation and taxes. I call this *going broke safely*.

You don't need to be a rocket scientist to know that we live in a world of risk; we always have and always will. Without risk, there would be no reward. Risk is basically uncertainty and the chance of a loss.

When you think about it, risk is really a lifetime concept that shows up all over the place. It could also take the form of loss of health, damage to your vehicle, a fire, a lawsuit, loss of a relationship, a foreclosure, or a loss due to greedy relatives. Perhaps one of the greatest risks of all is not being financially independent in your old age. However, when most people think of risk these days, they tend to think of financial risk. As you can see in table 6.1, it can take several forms.

Table 6.1 Investment risks

Type	Description
Market risk	This is the volatility of the financial markets. Your portfolio can lose money because of general market conditions, which may have nothing to do with your particular stock, bond, or mutual fund. Until the asset is sold, it is only a paper loss (or gain).
Inflation risk	Unlike market risk, losses from inflation are not paper market fluctuations—they are forever.
Economic risk	Changes in the global economy can affect your portfolio, your income, your neighborhood, and specific companies.

Table 6.1 (*continued*)

Liquidity risk	Those who have owned real estate, a limited partnership, or even a thinly-traded municipal bond know about this one. These types of investments may be hard to sell quickly at a fair price.
Credit risk	The company in which you own stock or the company or country to which you have loaned money can go under or fail to repay the bond principal and interest it owes you. Think Enron, Greece, or Detroit.
Interest-rate risk	If interest rates go up, the value of bonds and some types of stock can go down. If you need your money before the maturity date, you lose.

Risks are unavoidable. Trying to avoid the risks of owning stocks or real estate by keeping your money in the mattress may result in running out of money at an old age (or even losing your stash in the event of a fire, burglary, or flood if you literally put it under the mattress). On the other hand, investing for growth to avoid running out of money at an old age or to hedge inflation creates a different risk of losing money if an investment goes south. So, if you cannot avoid risk, all you can do is manage it by first identifying and measuring the severity and likelihood of it. Then you can transfer it, accept it, or try to minimize it.

Life insurance, homeowners insurance, health insurance, annuities, etc. are common risk-management tools. You are managing that risk by transferring it to a third party in exchange for a premium. In the investment arena, you generally accept the investment risks listed in table 6.1, but you try to minimize them through research, delegation, and above all, diversification.

All too often, people get burned by taking the wrong approach to managing investment risk. They start with a focus on hot investments when they should have covered their bases first, such as adequate homeowners and auto insurance, health and disability insurance, wills, etc. It looks something like figure 6.1, and as you can see, it doesn't take much to knock you down. Just ask those who speculated in the last housing bubble!

Figure 6.1 The wrong way to invest and manage risk

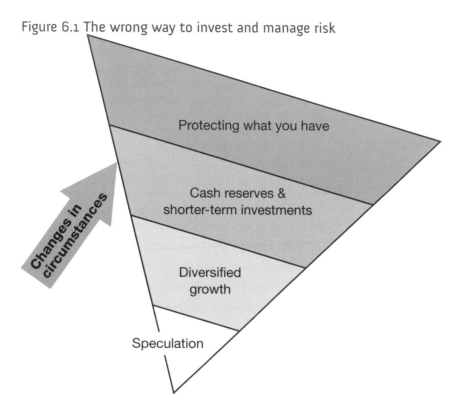

It's just common sense that you can better afford to lose money on a speculative investment or one with a lot of leverage (debt) if you have a solid foundation, as shown in figure 6.2. Changes in circumstances are less likely to topple your financial security.

Types of Investments: The Fuel for Your Journey

Okay, since there are no guarantees out there, how do you reach the potential returns in the examples of previous chapters? You put your

Figure 6.2 The proper way to invest and manage risk

Financial Independence Assets to work in a blend of two broad categories: loanership investments and ownership investments.

Loanership investments are considered more secure, but they are highly subject to inflation risk. It is where you loan money to someone else in the form of bank CDs, mortgages, Treasuries, bonds, and insurance annuity contracts. The people or organizations that borrow the money pay a fixed interest rate and promise to pay you back at a certain time or on demand. These organizations usually lend your loanership dollars to someone else at a higher interest rate or convert them into ownership investments.

Ownership investments are direct investments in businesses or income-producing assets, such as real estate. They have less certainty, more risk, and more potential reward.

There are many types of loanership and ownership investments.

Stocks, Bonds, and Mutual Funds

While there are some good ways to build Financial Independence Assets, such as owning and growing a business or developing a portfolio of rental real estate, my focus will be upon what I know best and what is commonly available and easy to implement for most people: diversified portfolios of financial assets, such as stocks and bonds and mutual funds or exchange-traded funds (ETFs) that own them. For now, I'll simply refer to mutual funds and ETFs as funds.

A typical fund might have three hundred to one thousand different holdings in its portfolio. While this limits the upside of owning a handful of winning stocks, it provides a higher degree of safety, as one company with problems cannot wipe out your portfolio. However, the fund could be subject to market risk and the daily ups and downs of the financial markets. This market risk is because the value of every company is calculated daily, and sometimes by the second, based upon the supply and demand for that particular company at any given moment on the stock exchanges. Shareholders have the right to be cashed out within three business days, based on their pro rata share of market value of the holdings in a fund. Daily price fluctuations in fund shares are the price mutual fund owners pay for this liquidity. This daily fluctuation creates the perception of risk, yet illiquid home or rental properties would probably fluctuate just as much if there were instant "appraisals" based on millions of real buyers and sellers every hour.

Stocks are basically shares of a business. *Corporate bonds* are IOUs to businesses. *Government bonds* are IOUs to a governmental entity. And *mutual funds* are pools of these. Some mutual funds are *actively managed* by a team that selects individual stocks or bonds. Others are passive, or called *index funds,* in which the stocks or bonds are pooled together to resemble an index, but they are not actively researched or traded as conditions warrant. Both types of mutual funds—actively managed and index—have their advantages, disadvantages, advocates, and detractors. My firm has had good results using a mixture of both types. That's all I'm going to say about them here, because the purpose of this book is to help you with the big picture.

There are literally thousands of mutual funds and ETFs, but they fall into a few broad categories of how they invest and their risk levels.

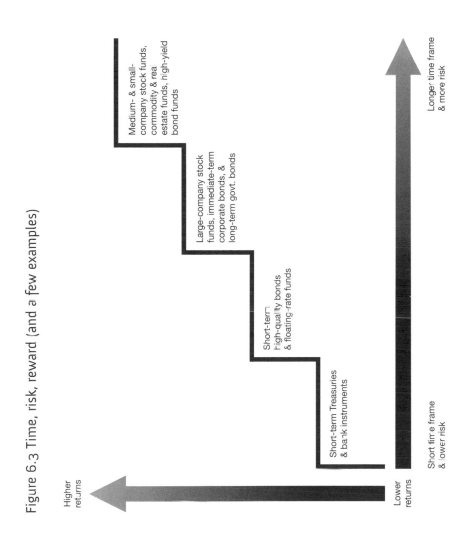

Figure 6.3 Time, risk, reward (and a few examples)

How do you know which asset classes to use? Obviously, a mixture would be prudent. That's where the professional art of asset allocation comes into play. An evenly divided mixture of asset classes won't get you too far because it would result in a heavier weighting of riskier assets. It's kind of like baking a cake: if you put equal amounts of every ingredient into the mix, you would have a very salty disaster in your oven!

The whole theory of asset allocation is that the *mixture* of what you have is more important than whether you owned stock A or bond B. "Modern" Portfolio Theory (MPT), going back to Nobel Prize winner Harry Markowitz in the 1950s, implies that for any given return there is an optimal portfolio mixture that potentially achieves that return with the least amount of risk possible. Using thousands of data points, this optimal portfolio mix can be visualized on a graph of the so-called "efficient frontier," which contains the best of all the possible return-risk combinations.

Figure 6.4 The efficient frontier

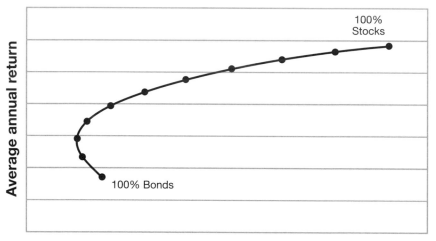

With modern computing power and data on many asset classes, it is possible to model what happens with the risk and reward of various mixtures. The simple model in figure 6.4 shows only two generic asset classes—large-company stocks and US government bonds. Note what happens when just a little amount of stocks is mixed in with bonds. The return goes up *and* the risk decreases. The results are even more dramatic when various mixtures of other asset classes—such as international stocks and bonds, commodities, and real estate—are added. The efficient frontier curve shifts to the left.

How can conservative assets, such as government bonds, be made safer and have a higher return by adding something more risky to it, like stocks? The answer is actually very straightforward. Asset classes react to market and economic conditions differently. They zig and zag: gold goes up and bonds go down on inflation fears, for example. In layman's terms, asset allocation tries to pair the zigs and zags against each other; in technical terms, it means pairing the negatively correlated assets with each other.

Figure 6.5 Correlation between asset classes

 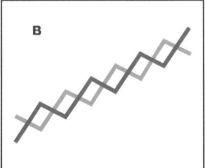

A. Positively correlated (not good); B. Negatively correlated (good).

So, back to the question of how to create your portfolio. Like baking a cake, my suggestion is to start with a lot of flour (bonds), then add sugar (large-company stocks), and then the other ingredients. The further you are from retirement, the less flour. But as you approach retirement or are in retirement, an all-flour (all-bond) mix is not appropriate, either. Remember, you could be retired for a long time. If you really want a mixture that balances your risk tolerance with your need for a decent return, you might want to hire a professional baker—an independent fee-only financial advisor who isn't trying to sell you his or her own brand of ingredients. Short of that, here are some rough guidelines:

Table 6.2 Possible asset allocations for time frames

Years to retirement	Bonds*	Stocks†	Historical long-term average annual return‡
30	20%–30%	80%–70%	9.0%–9.5%
20	30–40	70–60	8.5–9.0
10	40–60	60–40	7.5–8.5
5	50–60	50–40	7.5–8.0
0	60–80	40–20	6.5–7.5

* Should also include a mix of short- and longer-term, corporate, high-yield, and foreign bonds

† Should include mostly large-company stocks but also midsize- and small-company stocks, and about 20% of the allocation should include international funds

‡ Includes simple asset allocations for US large-cap stocks and long-term government bonds since 1926

Risk and Reward: Real Numbers over Time

As I edit this chapter in September 2013, the Dow and the Standard and Poor's (S&P) 500 are in record territory, greatly surpassing their October 2007 all-time highs. People are feeling better about stocks, and they have started coming back into the market. However, there is still a persistent fear of the market since the dot.com stock boom crashed in 2000. The resulting Great Recession has spooked many investors, and they are falling into a classic behavioral finance trap called "the experience effect," in which the recent past distorts perceptions about the present and the future. (It happens in reverse during bull markets.) The perception of the 2000s as "the lost decade" continues to shape the thinking that people can't make money in the stock market. We continue to get push back from clients when we use what we consider modest return assumptions of 4–7 percent for our retirement planning projections. So, let's put these concerns into perspective.

Although commonly used in media scorecards, beware of calendar years and official decades because they are artificial and misleading. In 2009, for example, the stock market as represented by the S&P 500 (an index of the five hundred largest companies) turned in a very respectable 27 percent return. But that doesn't tell the story of a first-quarter decline of nearly 10 percent and a stunning 45 percent return since March 1, and it certainly doesn't tell the nerve-wracking story of the 42 percent plunge from September 2008 through February 2009.

And what about the 2000s, the so-called "lost decade"? From January 1, 2000 to December 31, 2009, the annualized return for stocks was −0.95 percent, but bonds as represented by the Barclays Aggregate Index had a total return of 7.30 percent. Not exactly a lost decade for bond investors. And during that decade, there were five good years for stocks. It all depended upon your timing.

What if we looked at *rolling* averages for twelve-month periods and ten-year periods instead? My portfolio-management team looked at various data sources going back to 1926 and started a new year every month starting in 1927 and a new decade in 1936. This gave us 1,033 rolling "years" and 925 rolling "decades." Now those are a lot of years and decades!

As you might expect with more starting and ending points, the results were *much* better on average than artificial calendar years and decades. Stocks averaged over 11 percent per year, bonds almost 6 percent, and a 60-40 blend of stocks and bonds averaged over 8.5

percent. Other returns for different mixes are shown in table 6.2. Taking a longer view reinforces the idea that one shouldn't make all future assumptions based on the 2000s.

For stocks, at least, maybe the pundits were right about the 2000s being the lost decade. But how will that help you set assumptions as you plan for your future? Should you really plan three decades of retirement around what just happened or around partisan budget debates? Looking at long-term performance over rolling periods suggests that you shouldn't, any more than you should have made plans to live large off the huge stock returns from the '80s and '90s.

Calendars are a wonderful tool to help us grasp the abstract concept of the future, so use them to set goals and deadlines. But forget about using their artificial boundaries to describe the past when making your planning assumptions—that's like trying to read the highway signs through the rearview mirror after you've already passed them.

Real Estate and Gold

Some readers are going to wonder if I have forgotten to mention real estate and gold as investment options. The short answer is no: I briefly mentioned rental real estate earlier in this chapter as an ownership investment. If you have "The Four T's"—the time, temperament, talent, and tools—to acquire rental properties and manage them, more power to you. It can be a nice addition to your overall diversification. However, the reality is most people do not. The real estate crash of 2008 has also demonstrated that no investment goes up forever, and when times are tough, liquidity dries up. We allocate real estate to a percentage of our clients' portfolios by using mutual funds that invest in real estate investment trusts (REITs), which hold real estate rather than stocks and bonds. They most often have holdings that the average person couldn't afford to own, such as prime commercial property, hotels, shopping centers, office buildings, long-term care facilities, etc., both in the US and abroad.

And for gold? Its proponents insist that it is a good inflation hedge, but that isn't always so. It has a mixed record. My team looked at the price of gold, inflation, rates, and stocks with their dividends included, starting in August 1971 when our currency was taken off the gold standard.

Over the very long run (forty-one-and-a-half years), both gold and stocks have been good investments. Gold did well in the 1970s, when we went off the gold standard, and in the 2000s. But there are other times when stocks and inflation grew more.

For your retirement journey, you are going to need fuel—investments that can provide you with liquidity and income. You could probably take care of the liquidity part by investing in gold through exchange-traded funds (ETFs), but the bottom line is that gold does not produce an income. Unlike owning shares of businesses through stocks, gold does not add value to anything, except perhaps to a tooth crown or a ring finger. It can be an emotional investment, and sometimes and ideological one. Sure, buy a little if you wish as an inflation hedge, but don't bet your retirement on it. If you had done so in 1980, you probably wouldn't have stayed retired very long.

Social Security

If you really want to talk about gold for your journey, one of the most golden fuels you can have is Social Security. Whereas the investments I described earlier are like traditional fossil fuels, Social Security and some inflation-adjusted public pensions are like hydrogen-powered fuel cells. In chapter 1, I briefly covered the importance of Social Security. However, if reforms aren't put in place, benefits could be scaled back by 23 percent by the year 2033, according to the 2013 Social Security Trustees Annual Report.[21] But even then, Social Security remains a very good deal.

I've mentioned longevity several times. It is another risk you face on your retirement journey in the sense that you could outlive your Financial Independence Assets if you live a long time. It just stands

Figure 6.6 OASDI income, cost, and expenditures as percentages of taxable payroll (under intermediate assumptions)

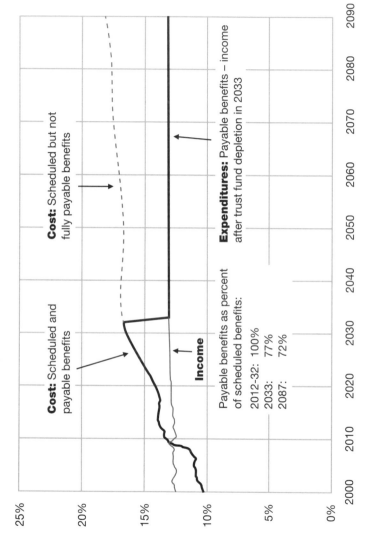

Source: 2013 OASDI Trustees Report[22]

to reason that by pulling $2,000 per month less from your portfolio to account for your Social Security payment, your portfolio is going to live a lot longer. This is especially true in a down market, when you may need to liquidate assets when prices are low. But wait—remember that Social Security has a COLA attached to it, and while this may not completely track your cost of living in retirement, at least it increases. This makes it superior to most annuity contracts and private-sector company pensions. Remember the earlier anecdote about my dad?

First, Some Alphabet Soup

Before we dive too deep into Social Security, let's go over some terminology. You can find more elaborate explanations at www .socialsecurity.gov. The *primary insurance amount (PIA)* is determined when you reach age sixty-two. A lot goes into calculating this, including your *average indexed monthly earnings (AIME)* over the past thirty-five years. The AIME is tinkered with what are called *bend points* to arrive at your primary insurance amount, the PIA. From age sixty-two until your *full retirement age (FRA),* your PIA is adjusted by the amount of COLAs granted to existing Social Security recipients. (Are you confused yet? If so, you are normal!) The FRA is age sixty-six for those born in 1954 or earlier. It increases two months per birth year to 1960, when the FRA is age sixty-seven.

When to Apply?

The big question for many people approaching their retirement journey is when to take Social Security benefits. Some are worried that Social Security won't be there when they retire or during retirement. Every year, the trustees of the Social Security Trust Fund issue new solvency reports based on actuarial projections. Their latest findings (as illustrated in figure 6.6) show that Social Security will most likely be there as we know it until the year 2033.[23] Beyond that, benefits will possibly be 75 percent less. Several factors go into when to claim, such as your health status, life expectancy, need for income, whether you plan to work, and possible survivor needs.

I'll make the claiming decision very easy for you: start as late as possible! This is especially true if you plan to work full- or part-time between age sixty-two and your FRA, which could be age sixty-six or sixty-seven. First of all, if you apply before your FRA, you will take an immediate 25 percent cut in benefit that lasts forever; all future COLAs will be based on only 75 percent of your starting amount. Second, if you apply before your FRA and you work, you will lose $1 in benefits for every $2 you earn over $15,120 in 2013. Your benefit will be adjusted at your FRA, but from the perspectives of income tax and future Social Security benefits, you will earn more in the long run if you can wait—especially if you don't need the money.

Better yet, if you can wait for your FRA of sixty-six or sixty-seven to age seventy, you will get an 8 percent increase in benefits every year. That's a return that is hard to beat, especially when those benefits include a COLA. We have run the numbers for our clients many times, and it almost always makes sense to either work longer or take income from a portfolio to postpone taking Social Security.

Assume your FRA amount is $2,000 at age sixty-six and Social Security pays a 3 percent COLA. Which would you rather have: $1,500 per month at age sixty-two that grows to $1,900 at age seventy? Or nothing right away, but at age seventy start collecting $3,344? While it is tempting to take the benefits early, the breakeven point of waiting is age seventy-eight. By then, your cumulative benefits will always be greater every year than if you had taken benefits early.

Do you have poor health and think that you will not live that long? What about your spouse? If you die, he or she gets the greater of either his or her benefit or yours. So, if your spouse's benefit is less than yours, it makes even more sense for you to defer taking benefits. Would you want your spouse to get a benefit that compounds with a COLA on a higher number or a lower number? (Remember, in chapter 1 we looked at actuarial figures. A nonsmoking couple age sixty-five has a 50 percent chance that at least one partner will live to age ninety-two.) Using my example above, would you want your spouse to have monthly income of $3,332 or $5,864 at age eighty-nine?

One way to have your cake and eat it, too, is to use the "file and suspend" strategy. This works well when couples are close in age and one spouse has earned significantly less. The higher-earning spouse files at age sixty-six but suspends receiving benefits until age seventy. This enables his or her ultimate benefit to increase by 8 percent per year to age seventy. The lower-earning spouse files for a spousal benefit, which would be half of the higher-earning spouse's age sixty-six benefit.

As an example (assuming no COLAs), John and Mary are sixty-six. John's PIA is $2,000; Mary's is $800. John files and suspends benefits at sixty-six; Mary claims her spousal benefit of $1,000, which is half of John's full benefit. At age seventy, John claims his benefit of $2,640, and Mary continues to collect her $1,000 spousal benefit. As an added wrinkle, John at age sixty-six could claim a spousal benefit on half of Mary's $800, then switch to his own record at age seventy.

Three key points here regarding the file and suspend strategy: (1) this strategy can only be used when the higher-earning spouse is at FRA, (2) seek competent advice before employing this strategy, and only after you know for certain what your actual FRA benefit will be, and (3) whether this strategy will be available when you retire is unknown, so don't base your entire retirement planning on this extra source of inflation-adjusted income.

Getting Help

The Social Security website (www.socialsecurity.gov) has benefit calculators and a wealth of information. Our clients have reported that applying online is also easy. I encourage you to meet with a Social Security representative as you approach the decision of when to apply; they can help you estimate your benefits and tell you the amount you are entitled to receive now. However, they cannot project future benefits through scenario planning, and they cannot help you with innovative strategies designed to maximize benefits. That's where a qualified financial advisor with robust (and not-so-cheap) software can help you.

Other Sustainable Fuels for Your Journey

Pensions

As with Social Security, a pension is a monthly income for life. Unfortunately, for many workers in the private sector, they are quickly becoming a thing of the past. These take the form of defined benefit plans, where the amount of the retiree's *benefit* is predetermined by a formula based on income and years of service. The employer takes on the investment and longevity risk, which often requires larger payments into the plan compared with a defined contribution plan, such as a 401(k) or profit-sharing plan. Under the defined contribution plan, the amount of the *contribution* is predetermined. The employer and the employee can contribute to it, and the results of those contributions are used to provide a benefit at retirement that is not guaranteed. In effect, employers are shifting the investment risk, the longevity risk, and—to some extent—the amount of the required contributions to the employees. This trend is happening in the public sector as well, where the retirement benefits are a combination of a defined benefit and a lump sum that can be rolled over to an individual retirement account (IRA) or be used to purchase an annuity, which will be discussed later in this chapter.

Most public pensions have COLAs, which is good for the retiree, but it requires a huge amount of money to be paid in (by taxpayers) during the working years. Many public pension funds are currently underfunded, meaning that not enough money has been set aside to cover future benefits.

Public and private pension plans can pay out more than one could safely withdraw from a defined contribution plan because they pool the risk. If a pensioner dies early, the amount of money needed to support him or her can be used to support other retirees who live longer. But because we are all living longer, that's now one of the reasons that pension funds have so many unfunded liabilities. In addition, pension plans give you more than one option for distribution. If you want the highest-possible monthly benefit, choose the life-only option (under federal law, you will need your spouse's written consent for this.) When you die with the life-only option, that's it; the pension party is over. More commonly, retirees elect to add their spouses for life but at a lower monthly payout rate. Others roll the entire account balance over to an IRA.

Which option should you take? There is no standard advice. It all depends upon your health and that of your spouse, assets, income sources, and whether you want to leave a family or a charitable legacy.

Some people nearing retirement are approached with a *pension-max* strategy by insurance agents. This involves taking the higher-paying life-only option and using some of the extra income from it to purchase a life insurance policy to protect the spouse when the pensioner dies. This places a huge amount of risk on the surviving spouse. In the proposals we have reviewed for second opinions, this rarely pencils out, especially with pension plans that have COLAs. Don't do it unless the odds are very high that your spouse is going to die before you do and you are convinced that you have more than enough life insurance and other assets.

Should you take the annuity payments from a pension or take a lump sum and roll it into an IRA? Again, that depends. If your company's pension plan is not in good financial health or if it does not have a COLA, it might be better to do the rollover. On the other hand, some pension plans are very strong. For example, I practice in Oregon, and we generally discourage members of the Oregon Public Employee Retirement System (PERS) from rolling funds into an IRA. Because of the COLA, generous formula, and pooled longevity risk-sharing of this program, it would be hard for us to match that unless we had above-average investment results year in and year out. That said, some split the difference by taking a smaller annuity and rolling the rest to an IRA. Often, the reasons are due to failing health, the desire to leave an inheritance, not needing all of the taxable pension income immediately, or the spouse having a good pension.

This is a big decision with huge long-term consequences for you, your spouse, your children, and your favorite charities. Whatever you decide to do, don't make this decision in a vacuum. Seek advice, and if the *only* advice you get is to roll it to an IRA, look for another advisor.

Tax-Deferred Vehicles

I've mentioned IRAs and 401(k)s in passing. Employees of educational institutions and other nonprofits have 403(b) accounts, which are very similar to 401(k)s in many respects. Finally, some public employees have access to tax-deferred compensation accounts. People often confuse them as investments, or fuel for the journey. They aren't. They are simply tax-deferred vehicles in which to put the fuel or hold the investments. Much has been written on this topic, and a detailed review of it is beyond the scope of this book.

But I will say this. A reasonable balance of your assets in both tax-deferred and taxable accounts is desirable. Overall, I encourage you to lean more toward investing your long-term Financial Independence Assets into tax-deferred accounts because they will grow faster without the earnings being taxed.

If you are a younger reader and/or you are in a relatively low tax bracket, I encourage you to take advantage of a Roth IRA or the Roth option if your employer has one with its 401(k) plan. While your contributions will not be tax deductible, you get the benefit of tax-free compounding and *tax-free* withdrawals at retirement.

Annuities

An annuity is like a pension plan. You give an insurance company a lump sum of money, and it promises to pay you a guaranteed amount of money every month for the rest of your life—no matter how long you live, no matter what the financial markets do. Annuities are now being marketed as longevity insurance. Some even have COLA features—for a price. They are promoted by proprietary, commission-driven insurance agents on one end and by respected and credentialed fee-only financial advisors on the other. If you have the funds to purchase a large enough annuity, you could have your fixed living expenses covered for the rest of your life, and you won't have to worry about the stock and bond market or living too long.

But right now, that's the rub—it will take a lot of money in this low-interest-rate environment to purchase a decent income stream. That is because insurance companies invest mostly in high-quality bonds (with a few skyscrapers thrown in for good measure). The companies must make actuarial assumptions (the same ones pension plan actuaries must make) regarding life expectancy and investment earnings, plus a company profit component and, often, an agent commission.

As an example, a financially solid national company will accept $100,000 in April 2013 from a sixty-year-old male and promise to pay him $10,913 a year for life when he turns seventy. Effectively, the return on his initial $100,000 investment will have been 0.57 percent a year if he lives to age eighty. If he gets to age eighty-five, he'll have made 2.82 percent a year on his money. Once he gets to ninety, he'll have made 4 percent. From the examples elsewhere in this chapter, historically speaking, you can do better with your money investing in a mix of stocks and bonds.

One other thought. Annuities are attractive in this volatile investment world because of their guarantees and safety. They don't have the ups and downs and the market risk of the stock market, but remember that any guarantee is only as good as the issuer. The financial meltdown in 2008 showed us that not all insurance companies are better at managing risk than the rest of us. One notable example was AIG (American International Group, Inc.) which needed a massive government bailout. A company could be sound today, but if you are buying longevity insurance, thirty or forty years from now is a long time in this fast-changing world.

So what's in your tank for the journey? Is it enough? Ideally, it is a specially crafted blend of equities, bonds, guarantees (like CDs, Treasuries, or annuities), pensions, and Social Security. Like any cross-country trip, the amount and power of fuel depend upon how far you plan to go, your fuel efficiency, and bumps along the way. Let's look at some detours next.

Your Road Map Action Items

1. What is your comfort level with the different kinds of risk described in table 6.1? Would you rather sleep well now or eat well later?
2. Look at figure 6.2. Are your Financial Independence Assets concentrated in only one or two categories?
3. Look at figure 6.3. How does your asset allocation compare to the suggested ranges for your age?
4. Go to www.socialsecurity.gov and experiment with the online benefit calculators to see how postponing benefits might affect you. (Remember, the results are not adjusted for COLAs.)

Dealing with Detours

A truly happy person is one who can enjoy the scenery on a detour.

—Anonymous

You've planned, saved, and implemented most of my suggestions. You've given a lot of thought about your retirement vision in chapter 2. You've run some basic numbers from chapter 4 or hired an advisor to run the numbers for you. You're confident that you have enough. So, let your retirement journey begin!

Every trip has an element of surprise. That's what makes it an adventure. If you obsess about the unknown, then it's hard to relax and enjoy the trip. The other extreme is to just assume that everything will work perfectly, and when it doesn't, you aren't prepared to deal with bumps in the road or unanticipated detours. So to be truly confident about your retirement journey, you need to be prepared to deal with surprises along the way.

Lots of things can happen before and during your retirement journey—as the saying goes, "Stuff happens." Let's explore six potential detours, or roadblocks, that deserve your attention before beginning your journey: (1) health, (2) long-term care, (3) dementia, (4) boomerang children, (5) procrastination, and (6) financial noise.

Detour 1: Health

I outlined health and long-term care issues in chapter 1. Your retirement journey is all about making the most of the last third or so of your life, based on your vision of what that might be. At its essence, this portion of life is the one that leads to our journey's end, and often over a bumpy road with many expensive medical issues. Taking care of yourself with diet, exercise, and meaningful connections is the best way to approach retirement and keep much of your journey smooth and enjoyable.

But even among the most fit and health conscious, health problems can emerge out of the blue. Medicare, fortified with Parts A, B, and D supplements, is like having AAA Roadside Assistance as you go down the retirement highway. Medicare as we know it today is starting to change, so no matter what I write today, things will have changed by the time you read this. Therefore, meet with a good health insurance agent and seek contemporary advice as you enroll in Medicare at age sixty-five. Even though you may be healthy at the time of enrollment, the lowest-cost option may not be the best for you in the long run. We're all just one fall or expensive drug therapy away from a huge hit to our Financial Independence Assets.

Sadly, there can be an even more catastrophic health-related hit to retirement, as some people won't live to age sixty-five. Take a quick look again at chapter 5, option 2 to refresh your memory about how critical the preretirement years can be. Usually those approaching retirement are at the peak of their earning power and savings rate. This is especially true with empty nesters with both partners still working. A loss of the income, additional pension credits, health insurance, future Social Security benefits, and extra savings has a profound impact on the surviving partner's Financial Independence Assets.

Even though the kids may be out of the house, we encourage our preretirement clients to have adequate life insurance to insure their most valuable asset—the ability to earn an income. Usually a low-cost five- or ten-year level term policy does the trick. In fact, you'll be surprised at how reasonable the cost can be if you are healthy. The term length should be at least your remaining working years, perhaps a couple more as a hedge. To estimate the face amount, simply estimate your cumulative earnings for that time period.

Detour 2: Long-Term Care

One thing that Medicare does not cover is extended long-term care. As I said in chapter 1, you may not develop an expensive medical condition, but perhaps you will lose your ability to function well on your own, hopefully after you've had a long and fulfilling Phase 1 and Phase 2. Our most difficult task is to convince our clients to plan for long-term care. A new survey by the AP-NORC Center for Public Affairs Research confirms what we've known all along—aging Americans are in denial about the need to plan for long-term care. In fact, according to the study, three in ten would rather not think about getting older at all, and only a quarter predict it's very likely that they'll need help getting around or caring for themselves during their senior years.[24]

However, the odds are high that you will need some form of care. With a rapidly aging population, more families will be facing those responsibilities. Government figures show nearly seven in ten Americans will need long-term care at some point after they reach age sixty-five, whether it's from a relative, a home-health aide, assisted living, or a nursing home. On average, they'll need that care for three years.[25] Age, gender, mobility, existing health conditions, and your living arrangements can all have an effect on whether you will need long-term care.

The costs can be devastating to your Financial Independence Assets. The Genworth 2013 Annual Cost of Care Survey reports that it now costs over $75,000 per year for a semiprivate room. Of course, in-home care and assisted living are less, but skilled care in a private room is considerably more.[26] Whether you self-insure with sufficient assets, plan to draft a family member, or purchase long-term care insurance, the important thing is to come up with a workable plan should you become incapacitated. A good place to start is a very informative website, www.longtermcare.gov. Then seek the advice of an independent health insurance agent who isn't tied to any particular company. Yes, the agent might say that they work for a certain company but are independent and can show you options from other companies. But in reality, the advice won't be as objective and the variety of options not as broad compared to an agent who is truly independent.

The long-term care industry has changed dramatically in the past twenty years. At first, only a few companies offered coverage. Then as demand grew, other companies got into the business. Policies were underpriced and issued without much actuarial data or claims experience. Then a funny thing happened—people actually needed long-term care, and the companies realized just how expensive it was. A fair number of companies have exited the market by selling their book of business to the survivors, and now the survivors are raising their rates, often dramatically. Why? Because people really do file claims for long-term care expenses. That should tell you that these statistics about the need for long-term care are grounded in fact.

One of the positive developments is that the industry now has much better data about the length of claims and looks more favorably toward in-home care. We now know that a vast majority of claims are less than four years.[27] So, rather than selecting, say, a $100-per-day-for-life benefit, it would make more sense to select $200–$300 per day for four years. Another positive development is that some companies are offering more flexibility among spouses and partners, allowing one policy that costs less than two separate ones.

Yes, long-term care premiums are expensive, especially the longer you wait to purchase a policy. You may pay premiums for a long time and never get a dime back, but you probably don't think that way about homeowners or auto insurance. You are glad to have the coverage, and even more glad that your house didn't burn down or that you didn't have a major vehicle crash.

I am not saying that purchasing a long-term care policy is the solution in all cases. As I said earlier, you can address this potential detour in a combination of ways, but I have observed firsthand how financially devastating long-term care can be. I can also tell you about all the "Thank you so much for getting that policy for Mom" comments and notes from the children of clients receiving expensive care and how we have also seen it liberate clients to enjoy their journey.

There was one couple in particular, I'll call them Sally and Bob, who had a very comfortable Financial Independence net worth and excellent health. But when Bob retired at age sixty-two, they never went anywhere or did anything, even though they had shared their retirement dreams (which included travel) with us over the years leading up to retirement. After three years, they finally admitted that they were afraid to go on a cruise or pursue their other dreams because they might need some of their portfolio to pay for long-term care expenses down the road, and they thought that the insurance premiums were too expensive. When we showed Sally and Bob that just some of the dividends from their holdings were more than enough to cover the insurance premium, they agreed to get some coverage. Suddenly, they were going on cruises every year, traveling to Australia, spending every January in Arizona, and purchasing a new car. Later on, Bob developed a rare form of cancer and needed skilled nursing care for nearly a year before he passed away. The policy paid for much of the costs, and Sally's portfolio is still holding up nicely today.

What about Your Parents?

Sooner or later, most retirees must deal with an aging parent. The odds are high that you already know somebody who is. It could involve worry about them, driving them to medical appointments, postponing vacations, helping to pay for their long-term care expenses, or actually providing in-home care for them. In addition to the costs, parental care sometimes comes with a huge emotional and physical toll.

Families differ in how they deal with parental care. Some would have it no other way than to have Mom move in with them. Others want Mom or Dad to live independently but then will provide a lot of help to make that possible. In other situations, the parents don't want to be a burden of any kind, so they move into assisted living if they can afford to do so. There is no right way that applies to every family, except to have a frank conversation before the need arises. If you think parental care will adversely affect your Financial Independence Assets, and your parents don't have the means to provide for their own long-term care, you should encourage them to apply for long-term care insurance. You may also want to revisit The Confident Retirement Journey Expense Analysis™ (worksheet 3.2) and revise your number as described in chapter 4.

Detour 3: Dementia

I'm not a gerontologist, internist, psychiatrist, or a medical doctor, but as a "portfolio doctor," I've seen firsthand what dementia—and especially Alzheimer's disease—can do to one's family and portfolio. I've also seen the good side when clients admit they might be affected by dementia and other related problems.

Dementia in its various forms is more common than you might think. The Alzheimer's Association estimates that between 2.6 million and 5.1 million Americans over the age of sixty-five have some form of dementia. About one-third of people age eighty-five and older (32 percent) have Alzheimer's disease.[28] For many of us, it's not a question of *if* but *when*.

So what can you do to protect yourself, your family, and your wealth if dementia starts affecting you? Meet with an estate planning attorney to discuss a living trust. Unlike a will, which only takes effect upon your death, a living trust directs a successor trustee to handle the management of your affairs while you are still alive but incapacitated. Powers of attorney are also useful.

The time to take action is in the early stages of decline. Unfortunately, this is also a time of denial. We've noticed several clients in the early stages or even middle stages of decline that won't make the important decisions and seek help, even if they have a living trust and/or a power of attorney. The following are true stories of three clients and what they did (their names and backgrounds have been changed to protect their identities).

George

"George" was a retired, high-level executive who was used to giving orders to large numbers of people. Even before we observed any signs of memory loss, he had compiled a "user's manual" for his wife, which included everything from how to drain the lawn sprinklers in the fall, to the automobile maintenance schedule, to instructions to call my office about any financial questions.

George eventually started slipping in conversations, often forgetting what I had told him just days earlier or what he had told us. Then one day, he did something I never expected: he brought his wife and daughter into a regularly scheduled update meeting and instructed me to remove his name from their account. "I've been diagnosed with Alzheimer's," he explained. "I'm fine now, but I'm starting to slip up now and then, and I don't want anybody to take advantage of me later." That same day, all three of them met with their family attorney to remove George as a trustee of his living trust and appoint his daughter as a cotrustee with her mother. Then they did the same at the bank.

Talk about courage! About a year later, George started going downhill very fast. He died three years later in a care facility, and his family members were able to focus on enjoying their time with him, each other, and life. The family finances were managed without interruption or irrational instructions, and his widow remains financially secure today. And, by the way, he had a long-term care policy, which helped pay his $4,000-per-month nursing home bill.

Mary

"Mary" is a retired professional and a very successful investor. In fact, investing is a passionate hobby of hers, consuming at least an hour each day on the computer. Her husband has been totally uninvolved with family finances. She has a thoughtfully constructed portfolio and has done quite well on her own. About three years ago, Mary sought us out to manage her portfolios. When I asked why, I once again was privileged to witness foresight and courage. "I've just been diagnosed with Alzheimer's," she explained. "I'm starting to not trust my own judgment. I don't want to do anything stupid with our investments."

We all agreed that one of the best things Mary could do was keep her mind engaged, so we carved out a small amount of her assets as a hobby account for her to continue managing. It only lacked an extra zero on the bottom line, and she could afford to lose it. She turned her serious money over to us.

Lately, I've had to explain things repeatedly. Mary's husband is worried, but once again, Mary is showing courage and wisdom. She recently gave her son power of attorney, and he now attends our update meetings. The side benefit is that the son is getting a quick education from us on wealth management and will be in a much better position to handle a large inheritance when it eventually arrives.

Susie

"Susie" was somewhere in the early-to-moderate decline phase when she suddenly became a widow. Her husband had been a very successful business owner who controlled everything with an iron grip, and he left her a very large estate. The grief, stress, as well as medical and family issues seemed to accelerate her decline. Her two adult children aren't very good with money, except at spending it. Susie is still cognizant most of the time, but she just isn't interested in money unless she is giving it away. However, she had the good sense to hire a trusted advocate (recommended by her attorney) who pays her bills, manages the cash flow, visits her regularly, and coordinates things between the handyman, accountant, attorney, and us. Things would be an absolute mess if Susie hadn't taken this step.

The Common Thread

All three of these individuals have two things in common: they had good estate plans, and they relied upon professionals for financial advice. But most importantly, they had the courage and common sense to overcome the denial often associated with dementia. It wasn't easy, but they did it. As a result, their financial futures are secure, and their families have less stress.

However, for some, dementia will hit too quickly before the person has the competence to pass the baton. Therefore, it just makes sense to start building a deeper bench and have a serious discussion now with your family and advisors about how you would want to see things unfold if Alzheimer's or other forms of dementia strike you or your spouse. What are the trigger points or warning signs? Who will take over, and under what circumstances? You have control now—use it to have at least some control over your future.

Detour 4: Boomerang Children

One of the realities of the postcrash economic downturn is that more adult children need their parents to help them out financially. The chances are that you know of friends, neighbors, or relatives where this is happening. I am seeing this happen with a growing number of clients, and it usually takes two forms: (1) moving back in with Mom and Dad (the "boomerang" child) or (2) outright gifts for home down payments, cars, loan payments, gifts to grandchildren, tuition for grandchildren, or even cell phone bills.

Either way, they can be described as *KIPPERS* (kids invading parental pockets and eroding retirement savings). Not many families can withstand a long-term drain on assets that likely already took a blow during the 2008–2009 market meltdown.

Although the trend started in the mid-1980s when the term *boomerang child* was first known to be used, it has clearly accelerated for economic reasons. Having your children return to the safety net of your home can be a wonderful time of family closeness, but it can also create personal, marital, and financial stress.

It's no big deal if your adult children are turning to you for help for the first time because of a financial emergency. Stuff happens, especially in this economy. But it becomes problematic when they don't move out or they repeatedly line up for gifts or loans (that in most cases end up being gifts). Over the years, many of my clients have taken advantage of the annual gift exclusion, currently at $14,000 per parent per beneficiary, as a nice way to reduce the size of their taxable estates. Unfortunately, some of the adult children and grandchildren now have a sense of entitlement and dependency on those gifts at a time when their parents' real estate values and portfolio values are lower.

Figure 7.1 Percentage of young adults living at home 2005 & 2011

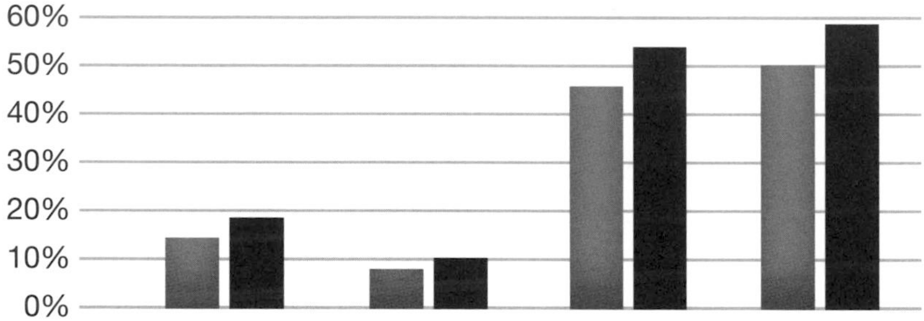

	Men 25–34	Women 25–34	Men 18–24	Women 18–24
2005	14%	8%	46%	50%
2011	19%	10%	53%	59%

Source: Data from US Census Bureau[29]

Part of the problem may be that for some families, the kids have no clue about their parents' financial situation. They don't grasp how much retirement costs and what it takes to adequately save for it. They grew up with a comfortable lifestyle in an era of plenty, and now their lifestyle isn't as high as it was when living at home before college. They see their parents living more comfortably than them and think, "Mom and Dad can afford to help me."

So, if you find yourself in this situation, here are five action steps:

1. *Update your retirement planning projections.* Financial advisors with good software can run a series of scenarios showing different annual gift amounts, savings rates, retirement dates, and retirement lifestyle costs. Once you have that, you will be in a better position for actions 2 and 3.

2. *Level with your kids.* Share as much of your current situation and planning projections as you feel comfortable. Who knows, it might even motivate them to start investing for their own futures.

3. *Just say no.* It's hard to say no to your children and see them experience some of the hardships you may have experienced. I know, because I am also a parent who has always wanted the best for my children. But I also know that many of the challenges and the delayed gratification I experienced over the years have helped to make me who I am today. There is a fine line between needs and wants, between helping and enabling!

4. *Help them restructure debts rather than simply bailing them out.* Then, teach them how to avoid new debt. One option is to match debt-reduction payments, with the understanding that they put away credit cards and live within their means.

5. *Make a loan a legitimate loan.* Plenty of websites have samples of promissory notes. Charge a fair interest rate and include reasonable terms that your child can afford.

As far as living with a boomerang? The most important thing you can do beforehand is have a serious discussion with your child and come to terms on the following items:

1. *Set a time limit.* Whether the boomerang child is getting a divorce, returning to school, or saving for a down payment on a house, set a time limit.

2. *Set goals and discuss expectations.* The odds are high that the boomerang child doesn't want to move back in any more than you want him or her to; it's hard and probably humiliating for your child as well. There may be valid reasons to move back in. Is it to pay off credit card debt? Recover from a bad relationship? Look for a new job? Talk frankly about the reasons behind this new living arrangement, and lay plans for the transition back to independence.

3. *Discuss rent.* For some parents, the mere mention of charging rent to a family member draws an incredulous reaction; but for other parents, charging rent helps prepare the boomerang child for living independently and helps with home finances. (I remember that my dad charged my older brother rent forty-five years ago.) According to Ask.Com's young-adult columnist Jackie Burrell, roughly half the nation's boomerang kids pay rent, ranging anywhere from $200 a month to the going market rate.[30] Some families start at one rate, then as an incentive for their children to move out, they raise the monthly rent by a predetermined amount as the months tick by. Others charge rent but set the money aside and present it as a nest egg when junior moves out.

4. *Agree upon rules and chores.* You are basically living with another adult, not a child, so it's unrealistic to set curfews. But you need to have rules about loud music, overnight guests, and alcohol or other substance issues. You also need to agree on a set of household chores, such as laundry, help around the house, cooking, yard work, and other chores. Otherwise, it's too easy to slip back into Mom-takes-care-of-everything

mode, which does nothing to foster independence and much to breed resentment.

5. *Make a contract.* Whatever the plan, discuss it and spell it out beforehand, and put it in writing. It can be really simple and no longer than the words used to describe these five points.

It's all about you and your own financial security. Love your kids, but do not sacrifice your own financial future by enabling KIPPERS. Like all parents, you have sacrificed many times over for your children. Now it's time to take care of *you*. They will still love you in the long run. Your children have decades to build their financial security, while you do not. Ironically, if you are not careful, you could end up depending on your children for financial help in your old age.

Detour 5: Procrastination

For many of us, procrastination—and its guilt—is the 800-pound gorilla in the room. (That's why it took me so long to start and finish this book!) Understanding why we do it and how to get around it is the first step to getting things done. Why would I list procrastination as a detour? For one thing, it may delay the start of your confident retirement journey. Remember the cost of one year of procrastination (table 5.1) in chapter 5?

But why does it matter, if you are already retired? Isn't one of the perks that you don't have a list of things to do? Unless your idea of a fulfilling retirement is just sitting around in a rocking chair all day, procrastination insidiously chips away at your retirement vision. Believe it or not, over the past thirty years, I have observed more procrastination among retired clients than those who are still working. They are the ones to drag their heels on projects that connote "should" or "ought": the important but not the urgent. These are things like getting their estate planning completed (see earlier discussion on dementia), deciding on long-term care, or just basic follow-through on the financial planning tasks we assign them. Sometimes, it is also the fun stuff, like booking a trip, or lifestyle-enhancing stuff, like getting hearing aids. Many retirees brag that they are so busy that they don't know how they ever got anything done when they were working. The mistake here is confusing activity/busyness with productivity.

Why is that? When you have a day job, you have to set priorities and schedule things. You are accountable for your time. You don't have all day to read the morning paper or get your workout completed. It goes beyond simple routines. All of us procrastinate because we haven't sold ourselves on the task or the project, such as seeing a financial advisor or getting a living trust. We don't understand the positive consequences of completing it, and the project can seem so overwhelming that we don't know where to start. Maybe we're reluctant to spend money on a lawyer, on hearing aids, or on a cruise because we haven't made it a priority or we're not confident that we can afford it.

Sometimes, procrastination is a valid strategy when other factors are not in place. It can make sense on really complex things that require a lot of thought, or when there is too much ambiguity. If so, admit it instead of letting it hang over your head and give you guilt and sap you of energy. Sleep on it, but set a date when you will deal with it. And remember, when it comes to financial and life planning, *it's all about progress, not perfection.*

Detour 6: Financial Noise

Speaking of being overwhelmed, many financial advisors notice a big change in some retirees once the retirement party is over and they return from the cruise. They now have a lot of time on their hands to watch the cable news channels and surf the Web. As a result, they worry more, lose their long-term perspective, and some start trusting what they see on TV more than they do the steady wisdom of the advisor that helped get them to retirement. This, too, can circle back to procrastination.

In many ways, investing is harder today than it was over thirty-two years ago when I started my practice. Back then, the challenge was *getting* information and being able to act upon it. It was expensive, slow, and always filtered through intermediaries. Today, the challenge is *too much* financial information and the tendency to overreact to it or become paralyzed by it.

In 1980, for example, *Money* magazine was in its infancy. You can now go to Google or Amazon and find thousands of books, magazines, newspapers, and websites devoted to investing and financial planning.

In 1980, there were 564 mutual funds; today (as of the end of 2012), there are 7,596 open-ended mutual funds in the US. These funds have a variety of share classes, such as "Class A" or "Institutional," which expands the total number of share offerings to 24,257. Plus, there are 1,194 exchange-traded funds that didn't exist in 1980 and 602 closed-end mutual funds.[31] Add all of these up and you get a whopping 26,093, or 8,796 without the separate share classes.

There was no Internet or financial TV shows in 1980, and there were very few cable stations. Now, CNBC alone hosts about fifty guests a day, many of whom are asked for their hot stock tips. Many of the broader networks and news shows contain regular segments on investments and financial planning, as do our newspapers, websites, and general magazines. At what point does all this information become just "financial noise"?

All of this overload and confusion can be divided into a spectrum:

DATA ➡ INFORMATION ➡ KNOWLEDGE ➡ WISDOM

So much of what is out there really falls into the data and information categories, kind of like the news. They may be timely, but they are not timeless. (Do you remember *exactly* what the Dow Jones index and the headlines were six months ago today?)

Data and information are noise. They crowd out knowledge, and knowledge without a sense of perspective and experience cannot be-

come wisdom. With all the financial noise these days, it is challenging to develop adequate knowledge and convert that to wisdom-based action. That's where a good professional can help, whether it is in law, medicine, accounting, or wealth management and planning. If I want medical data and information, I can easily find it, even at the grocery check stand. But if I want knowledge and wisdom (and good hands-on attention), I definitely want an experienced physician.

So, before you read that next financial magazine, surf the Web, or tune into that TV financial news show, spare yourself the overload and save some time and peace of mind by asking yourself the following questions from my financial-noise filter.

Ron's Financial-Noise Filter

1. *Will this information be obsolete and forgotten within a few hours, days, or weeks?* If yes, go do something more productive.
2. *Does this apply to me?* If not, skip to the next article. The hardest part about writing my weekly blog and quarterly newsletter is selecting a topic that has the broadest appeal, so I'll be the first to admit that not everything I write is relevant to every reader.
3. *Will this information give me peace of mind or increase my anxiety?* If it increases your anxiety, move on to something else. Good news rarely sells, and disturbing people is a basic fundamental of advertising.
4. *Can I do anything about it?* If not, don't worry about it.
5. *Will I do anything about it?* If not, then why waste your precious time and mental energy?
6. *How will this information get me closer to my financial and life goals?* Sometimes it can be mesmerizing to watch the stock ticker on one of the TV monitors in the gym, but how will knowing where the DOW is at any given moment change your life? And does that distract you from thinking about the

more important things in life or enjoying a good soundtrack with your headphones?

7. *Does the source know my circumstances and me?* If not, take all general advice—including this book—as only a starting point. All too often, I see the adverse results when people follow well-meaning general advice that wasn't appropriate for them because there were other mitigating facts or client objectives. (Frankly, the biggest frustration I have as a writer is trying to cover all the bases, yet keep it simple and relevant to as many readers as possible.)

8. *What is the source and its interests in promoting the information?* If it's to obtain more subscriptions, more viewers, more Internet hits, sales, higher ratings, etc., move along.

9. *Does this source have hands-on experience "in the trenches" providing financial advice and managing money, or is the source merely reporting about it?* When in doubt, put more trust in those with recent real-life experiences. As I mentioned in the Preface, it's one thing to write about it, it's quite another to know from experience how things work with real people with their unique circumstances.

10. *Is the source accountable if it is wrong?* If not, don't rely on it. Your licensed advisor providing specific advice to you for a fee is held to a much higher standard than a stock analyst's report, an Internet chat room, a TV talking head, or the author or publisher of any book or article!

Hopefully, these ten tips will help you stay confident and enjoy your retirement journey. By the way, this filter works well with other "news noise," too.

Life itself is a journey with many twists and turns. Retirement is no different. With luck, you may not need to deal with chronic or catastrophic health issues, aging parents, boomerang children, or the need to go into a long-term care facility. But you should be prepared, just in case. All of us constantly face the roadblocks of procrastination and the cacophony of financial noise. Just being aware of them is half the battle.

Your Road Map Action Items

1. Review your Financial Independence Assets as they relate to your number (from chapter 4). Do you have enough assets to self-insure against the potential costs of long-term care? If not, meet with an independent long-term care insurance agent to learn what it would cost to transfer this risk to an insurance company.
2. Discuss with your parents their wishes about how to handle their care as they age.
3. At what point will you "pull the trigger" and let someone else manage your financial affairs, should you start slipping mentally?
4. If you have adult children living at home, develop a plan to help them become independent.
5. The next time you find yourself getting sucked into financial noise, step back and focus upon something else.

CHAPTER 8

Beyond the Horizon
(Or When the Retirement Planning Rubber Meets the Estate Planning Road)

We're spending our children's inheritance.
—Bumper sticker on the back of an RV

At the beginning of chapter 4, I talked about three things that can happen if you don't know your number. There is also a fourth item that may apply to some people when estate planning goals conflict with the need to accumulate Financial Independence Assets. Knowing your number helps you prioritize between a secure retirement for yourself and an inheritance for your children.

Once you are on your journey, you most likely won't need guardians for your children. You do, however, need to update your estate planning and coordinate it with your retirement planning. All too often, people treat each in a vacuum and don't see how they relate to one another. To integrate these two, you need to ask yourself three critical questions:

1. Do I want to leave an inheritance? If so, how much?
2. Do I want to leave a charitable legacy? If so, how much?
3. How will these desires affect my retirement security?

I can't answer the first question for you, as it is deeply personal and familial. But, here is my three cents' worth. First, your desire to enjoy a financially comfortable retirement can conflict with a desire to give gifts and leave a legacy for your children, your grandchildren, or a charity. It has real financial implications, as would the purchase of a retirement home. You need to know how the cost of leaving an inheritance or giving gifts can affect your lifestyle. If your expenditures are modest, if you die early without prolonged health care expenditures, or if you have good investment results on your Financial Independence Assets, then no problem. But sometimes you can't control all of these. Your first responsibility is to take care of yourself so that later you don't become a burden on your children or on society.

Second, consider the age, health, and financial circumstances of each beneficiary. Some are doing quite well and won't need a large inheritance to survive. Some might blow it. Others will always need assistance due to their vocation, health, or circumstances. Treating each beneficiary equally is not always fair, and treating each beneficiary fairly is not always equal. And who knows, your children could be retired by the time your inheritance finally happens.

Third, if you do plan to leave an inheritance, consider an *appropriate* inheritance, not an absolute inheritance. What would you want your heirs to do with it? Try mentally spending each beneficiary's inheritance. After adding up the costs of buying a home, paying off their student loans, funding college savings plans for the grandchildren, seeding their Financial Independence Assets, and perhaps buying a country club membership, you might realize that the amount of their anticipated inheritance far exceeds what they could reasonably spend. Better yet, do what I did by asking your children what they would do with a hypothetical (or not-so-hypothetical) amount from an inheritance. The answers you receive may surprise you in a good way, or they may confirm your hunches about a spendthrift child. These exercises are not about cutting them out but about deciding how much to give so as not to hurt them.

I can also say from experience that some of our clients who have inherited money viewed the inheritance as a burden and sometimes a source of guilt because it came out of context and they did nothing to earn it. Also, the older ones, those over age sixty, seemed to be better stewards.

A predetermined charitable bequest can have the same financial impact on your retirement security as leaving money to your heirs, but most people bequeath only what remains when they die. And in many respects, it is easier to decide to leave money to charity if your children are doing well and you are passionate about certain causes.

Okay, so you decided to leave something to your heirs or to charity. How do you determine whether you can afford to do so? Although the intent of this book is to give you do-it-yourself confidence about retirement, this is an instance where you really should seek professional advice if you want a highly detailed answer. This is especially if your retirement cash flow is going to be tight. The steps I outlined for you in chapter 4 assume that you will eventually consume your Financial Independence Assets by the time you reach your projected age of death. If you simply plan to leave your heirs or a charity what remains at that time, then no problem. If you want to leave more and be certain that there will be an inheritance or charitable bequest, then you need a larger Financial Independence Number.

How much larger? In nominal (before-inflation) dollars, you would need to have an additional $1,000 of Financial Independence Assets per $1,000 of inheritance. Hopefully, you will put that money to work, which means that you really don't need to set aside the full $1,000. If you thought you could earn 5 percent after taxes and that you will live another thirty years, then you would only need to set aside $231 for a $1,000 inheritance.

Table 8.1 Present value of $1,000 at various rates

Years	2%	3%	4%	5%	6%
5	$906	$863	$822	$784	$747
10	820	744	676	614	558
15	743	642	555	481	417
20	673	554	456	377	312
25	610	478	375	295	233
30	552	412	308	231	174
35	500	355	253	181	130
40	453	307	208	142	97

Table 8.1 also shows what that $1,000 would really be worth in infla-tion-adjusted dollars. If you assume a 3 percent inflation rate for the next thirty years, your $1,000 gift would only have the purchasing power of $412.

What if you wanted to leave your heirs $1,000 in real (after-infla-tion) dollars? Then you would start with $1,000, and it would need to grow by the inflation rate. What if, for example, you assumed that inflation would average 3 percent per year for the next thirty years? Look at the future-value table (table 8.2) and go to the 3 percent col-umn again. For your heirs to receive the equivalent of $1,000 in to-day's dollars, you will need to have an extra $2,427 left over at the end of thirty years to give to him or her.

Like table 8.1 that shows present values, table 8.2 is also useful for other things. It can help you calculate how much money you might have in the future at different earnings rates. It can also show you the opportunity cost for expenditures and how spending $1,000 now on something frivolous could end up costing you $3,870 in twenty years at an assumed 7 percent earnings rate.

Table 8.2 Future value of $1,000 at various rates

Years	1%	2%	3%	4%	5%	6%	7%	8%	9%
5	$1,051	$1,104	$1,159	$1,217	$1,276	$1,338	$1,403	$1,469	$1,539
10	1,105	1,219	1,344	1,480	1,629	1,791	1,967	2,159	2,367
15	1,161	1,346	1,558	1,801	2,079	2,397	2,759	3,172	3,642
20	1,220	1,486	1,806	2,191	2,653	3,207	3,870	4,661	5,604
25	1,282	1,641	2,094	2,666	3,386	4,292	5,427	6,848	8,623
30	1,348	1,811	2,427	3,243	4,322	5,743	7,612	10,063	13,268
35	1,417	2,000	2,814	3,946	5,516	7,686	10,677	14,785	20,414
40	1,489	2,208	3,262	4,801	7,040	10,286	14,974	21,725	31,409

Making Intentions Happen

We are all terminal. At some point, your journey will end, and your assets will pass on to others. The question becomes who decides? If you have not done formal estate planning, your state of residence will decide for you based on what are called intestacy laws. Odds are you wouldn't like the result, and there could be a lot of unintended consequences, including unnecessary publicity, family discord, and possible estate taxes. If you have real property in more than one state, the situation gets even more complicated and expensive. So it boils down to a matter of control, and I'm willing to bet that if you have taken the trouble to read this book, you are the type of person who wants to take control of your life. Why not take charge over everything you have worked so hard to accumulate? Why not do what you can to create harmony among your heirs?

If you want to make life easier on your children and be certain that your assets are properly distributed when you die, then you need to have your thoughts documented in a will and/or living trust and in the beneficiary designations of your retirement plans and insurance policies. A very nice side benefit is that it will increase your confidence and enjoyment of retirement.

This is not a book about estate planning, but I have collaborated with good estate planning attorneys over the years, and I have seen what good planning can do. However, I have also seen the train wrecks that happen with poor or no estate planning. Many of those disasters occur by those trying do-it-yourself wills, putting everything in joint names with the children, or using attorneys that don't devote much of their practice to estate planning. Worst of all, unintended consequences can happen when your family and financial situation change but your estate plan is not updated. A child may have been full of promise at age sixteen but is now chemically dependent at age twenty-six when you are an empty nester. Or a daughter might now be in a bad marriage. Large and string-free blocks of money to either of them upon your death could make things far worse. You can't undo the consequences of bad or outdated planning when you are gone.

So, ask your financial advisor for the names of good estate planning lawyers. They won't be cheap, and you may never know the true value of their work, but your heirs will. I am not an estate planning lawyer, but I recommend you have your lawyer do at least the following for you:

1. *Draft a will or a living trust.* I'm more partial to living trusts because they are easier to amend and they can provide for financial management when you are incapacitated. A will only springs to life upon your death. Living trusts may also help you avoid probate and the public proceedings when you become incapacitated and need a court-appointed guardian. Also, if you have real property in more than one state, a living trust can help your heirs avoid multiple probate proceedings.
2. *Make certain the assets are properly titled.* You can't give away your spouse's assets through a will or a trust. A will or trust has no power over jointly-held assets and beneficiary designations. And a living trust without assets retitled into its name is practically useless.
3. *Coordinate the beneficiary designations of your retirement plan accounts, life insurance, and annuities.* These assets transfer by contract law, so a will or trust is powerless over them. You can, however, transfer ownership of a life insurance policy into the name of a living trust so that beneficiary designations can be more easily changed by the trustee should you become incapacitated.
4. *Draft a power of attorney.* When you are alive but incapacitated, this can be used as a backstop when all else fails. However, it often doesn't contain the strings and safeguards of a living trust. Most often, this is used for retirement plan assets that cannot be owned by a will or trust.
5. *Create an advance directive and a health care power of*

attorney. Under most state laws, this allows you to control in advance the type and extent of heroic measures that may be used to prolong your life. It also gives one or more individuals the power to make those difficult decisions if you cannot make them for yourself.

As I said, having a good estate planning lawyer is essential. But he or she should help you put the above items together as part of your team that includes financial and tax professionals. Your financial advisor can provide additional insights about you and your situation and ultimately may be the one to help with changes to asset titling and beneficiary designations. If you have business interests and a large estate, your tax professional and your financial advisor can collaborate with the attorney and run the numbers on tax-saving strategies that go beyond the scope of this book.

The most important thing you can do is put some thought into what you want. All the words and numbers that go into creating your estate plan won't do a lot of good unless they truly represent your desires. You have three kinds of legacies:

1. Family wealth (money and possessions)
2. Social wealth (philanthropy)
3. Personal wealth (your values)

What do you want to happen? What do you want your legacy to be? What do you want your assets to do for your children, grandchildren, and charitable causes? Don't worry about how it can be done— that's the job of your lawyer, accountant, and financial advisor. Your job is to give them your vision. Here is a chart to help you collect your thoughts:

Figure 8.1 The Confident Legacy Vision®

Key Ingredients of a Well-Thought-Out Estate Plan

Values	Personal, Family, Spiritual
Concerns & Goals	Family, Community, Health
Family	History, Dynamics, Needs, Talents, Financial sophistication of beneficiaries
Assets	Composition, Liquidity, Ownership
Other	Laws, Taxes, Growth rates

Your Family, Social, and Personal Legacy

The Confident Legacy Vision® is a registered trademark of Kelemen Advisory Associates, LLC. © 2013 Ron Kelemen.

Making Things Easier on Your Heirs

Your well-documented intentions should promote harmony among your heirs and make life easier for others when you are gone. However, you need to take one more important step: make it easy for your primary heirs to find your documents and other valuable assets. If you don't, it is like leaving your neighbor instructions to water the houseplants while you are on vacation but forgetting to give her the house key. Where is the key to your safe deposit box—and for that matter, in which bank is it located? Where are your insurance policies located? What about all your stuff in your digital world? These could include the following items:

- Online bank and brokerage accounts
- Photos
- Emails
- Social media accounts
- Music collections
- Frequent-flyer statements
- Credit card or other monthly statements

- Social Security statements
- Mortgage information
- PayPal accounts
- Budgets and expenditures
- Tax returns
- Medical records

How can you, a trusted family member, or your executor get access to them? More fundamentally, how would anybody even *know* what you have and where it's located? In the traditional paper world, sooner or later a box of photos or letters will be found or an account statement will show up in the mail to give the family member or executor a clue that an asset or liability exists. Where to begin getting a handle on this?

Start by making a digital inventory. Feel free to use the Digital Inventory worksheet in the Appendix (worksheet A.2) as a template or download a copy at www.ConfidentRetirementJourney.com. Prioritize your assets, putting your email access at the top of the list, as an email account is the key to much of our digital world. We need it to get into social media sites like Facebook or to make a travel reservation. Ever lose a password or user name? Many sites send that information to your email address of record and ask for an answer to a private question, such as your first dog's name. Therefore, the most important user names and passwords you should highlight are those of your various email accounts.

It won't do anybody much good unless they know where to find it. So tell a trusted person, such as the executor of your estate, the trustee of your living trust, or a trusted family member, where this inventory is located. I have also included a Just in Case worksheet in the Appendix (worksheet A.3), which enables others to act on your behalf if necessary. Beyond just the financial things, your heirs will greatly appreciate the ability to access your digital photos, just as they would have enjoyed the print versions before digital cameras became popular.

Finally, I highly recommend Carroll and Romano's excellent book *Your Digital Afterlife: When Facebook, Flickr, and Twitter Are Your Estate, What's Your Legacy?*[32] They also have a resource-rich website located at www.yourdigitalafterlife.com/resources. (My thanks to them for giving me permission to use their template as an example in this book and on *The Confident Retirement Journey* website, www.ConfidentRetirementJourney.com.) Another useful resource is www.thedigitalbeyond.com, which has a list of online service providers to help you with this project.

Your Road Map Action Items

1. Schedule an appointment with an attorney who specializes in estate planning. Your financial advisor or tax professional can refer one or more to you. Don't worry that you don't have everything figured out yet. The attorney's questions will help you.
2. What kind of family and social legacies do you want to leave?
3. What do you think is an appropriate amount to leave your heirs? Are you willing to sacrifice your retirement lifestyle and security to leave an inheritance?
4. Review the Values, Concerns & Goals, and Family sections of figure 8.1. Jot down your initial thoughts and share them with your attorney.
5. Get started on the Digital Inventory and Just in Case worksheets in the Appendix (worksheets A.2 and A.3).

Ron Kelemen

CHAPTER 9

Let the Journey Begin!

It is good to have an end to journey toward;
but it is the journey that matters, in the end.
—Ernest Hemingway

Your Confident Retirement Journey™ starts with a vision, followed by the knowledge that you have addressed all the relevant factors to make your retirement journey a success. If you have time to focus upon only one chapter in this book, do so with chapter 2 to find your retirement vision. What is your definition of retirement? What is your vision of a perfect day in each of its three main phases? What are the most important things you would like to accomplish between now and retirement? Between retirement and when you die? Here is a summary of the broad things you should consider for your journey.

Figure 9.1 The Confident Retirement Vision®

Goals	When? Income level? Lifestyle? Philanthropy? Big purchases?
Obligations	Children, College, Debts
Resources	Pensions, Social Security, Investments

© 2013 Ron Kelemen.

Figure 9.1 (*continued*)

External	Variables, Inflation, Economy, Investment probabilities, Relevant laws
Other Factors	Health, Longevity, Taxes, Family, Legacy objectives, Financial sophistication of each spouse

The Confident Retirement Vision® is a registered trademark of Kelemen Advisory Associates, LLC. © 2013 Ron Kelemen.

Retirement planning is both a vision and a process. These items cannot be done in a day, or even a month, so I have included a more specific worksheet called The Retirement Readiness Process™ in the Appendix (worksheet A.4) to help you with your countdown.

Go forth with confidence in knowing that you have created your retirement vision and have taken the necessary steps to make your journey rewarding. Bon voyage!

(PS: Have fun!)

Your Road Map Action Items

1. Reread chapter 2 and complete The Second-Half Vision Focuser™ (worksheet 2.1) if you haven't already done so.
2. Review The Retirement Readiness Process™ in the Appendix (worksheet A.4) and get started on the first three items in the Now section.
3. Review the Getting Started worksheet in the Appendix (worksheet A.5) and decide which top-three action items you want to accomplish over the next month.
4. Visit some of the websites listed in the Internet Resources section in the Appendix.
5. Above all, get started and have fun doing it.

Appendix

Ron Kelemen

Worksheets

Worksheet A.1 The Second-Half Vision Focuser™

Your Life Goals for Your Second Half

Today's date:_____

Theme: _____

(Accomplishments, Health, Spiritual Goals, Relationships, Financial)

What are the most important things related to this theme that I want to accomplish between now and the end of my life?

Lifetime date (age ____)	
1.	
2.	
3.	
4.	
5.	
6.	
7.	
8.	
9.	
10.	

Worksheet A.1 (*continued*)

Ten-year benchmark date
1.
2.
3.
4.
5.
6.

One-year benchmark date
1.
2.
3.

Three-month benchmark date
1.
2.
3.

Three-year benchmark date
1.
2.
3.
4.
5.

One-month benchmark date
1.
2.
3.

The Second-Half Vision Focuser™ is a trademark of Kelemen Advisory Associates, LLC.

© 2013 Ron Kelemen. PDF form available at www.ConfidentRetirementJourney.com.

Worksheet A.2 Digital inventory

Assets of: _____ My Executor's Name: _____ Date: _____

Asset			Access			Wishes		
Name	Contents	Location	User name	Password	Instructions	Recipient	Notes
Computers or devices							
Email accounts							

Adapted with permission from *Your Digital Afterlife*, by Evan Carroll and John Romano.
© 2013 Ron Kelemen. PDF form available at www.ConfidentRetirementJourney.com.

Worksheet A.3 Just in case

If you were suddenly to become unavailable or disabled for a period of time due to illness, accident, or even an unexpected delay in returning from travel, it would be important for your loved ones to have the information they need to take care of you, and/or your day-to-day responsibilities.

This is a tool to gather vital, confidential information to enable others to act effectively on your behalf when needed.

Personal Information

	Person #1	Person #2
Full name, other names		
Date of birth and place		
Social Security #		
Father's name		
Mother's name		
Home address		

Worksheet A.3 (*continued*)

Medical Information

	Person #1	Person #2
Health insurance carrier and phone #		
Health insurance carrier and phone #		
Individual #		
Group #		
Physician		
Physician		
Dentist		
Medications		
Allergies		
Immunizations and dates		
Medical directive	Yes / No Location:	Yes / No Location:
Anatomical donor	On driver's license? Yes / No Registered? Yes / No	On driver's license? Yes / No Registered? Yes / No

Worksheet A.3 (*continued*)

Emergency Contact / Family List

Name	Relationship	Phone number(s)	Address

Worksheet A.3 (*continued*)

Who Takes Care of Your....

	Name	Contact information
Children		
Pets / animals		
Car		
Home maintenance / cleaning		
Landscape / yard work		
Dry cleaning		

© 2013 Ron Kelemen.

Worksheet A.3 (*continued*)

Other Contacts

Relationship	Name	Contact information
Business / employment		
Attorney		
Tax professional		
Insurance agent		
Financial advisor		
Executor		
Clergy		
Friend		

Worksheet A.3 (*continued*)

Location of Documents

• Identify the locations where you keep your documents.
• Be specific, providing addresses, contact information, and descriptions (as in "red binder on bottom shelf of bookcase in den at 123 Main St., Salem, Oregon").
• In the tables following this chart, enter the Location Key code and comments as needed.

Code	Location key
H Home	
W Workplace	
F Financial advisor	
T Tax professional	
A Attorney	
S Safe deposit box	
B-1 Bank	
B-2 Bank	

Ron Kelemen

Worksheet A.3 (*continued*)

Banking Records

List of accounts	
Checkbook / passbook	
Safe deposit box	
Safe deposit key	
Statements / cancelled checks	
Loans	

Worksheet A.3 (*continued*)

Legal Documents

Wills	
Powers of attorney	
Special bequests	
Trust documents	
Title insurance	
Deed	
Home inventory and insurance policy	
Life insurance policy	

Worksheet A.3 (*continued*)

Family Records

Birth certificates	
Adoption papers	
Guardianship / conservatorship	
Custody documents	
Social Security cards	
Proof of citizenship	
Marriage license	
Divorce decree	
Military service records	

Worksheet A.3 (*continued*)

Investments

Pension / retirement plans	
IRA accounts	
Mortgage documents	
Real estate deeds / titles	
Certificates of deposit	
Investment accounts	

Worksheet A.3 (*continued*)

Other

Important keys	
Vehicle title	
Antiques	
Jewelry	
Cash	
Passwords	
Funeral arrangements	
Personal journals	
Family photos	

Worksheet A.4 The Retirement Readiness Process™

Time before retirement	Action steps
Now	1. Analyze your situation or engage a qualified financial advisor to help you develop a custom-tailored plan of action.
	2. Begin addressing fundamental personal, financial, health, investment, and legacy questions.
	3. Begin making a list of what you will do during retirement (and the rest of your life!). (See The Second-Half Vision Focuser™.)
	4. Start developing more hobbies and outside interests.
Now and every 2 years	5. List your assets and liabilities using The Confident Retirement Journey Balance Sheet™.
	6. Estimate your current and future spending needs using The Confident Retirement Journey Approach™.
	7. Meet regularly with your financial advisor to review your situation, monitor your progress, and make necessary adjustments.
	8. Review your will, beneficiary designations, and other estate plan documents; make necessary changes.
	9. Review your buy-sell agreement if you own a business.
2–5 years	10. Take extended visits at different times of the year to potential vacation home locations.
	11. Start doing the many things necessary to increase the value of your business or practice.
18 months	12. Try living on projected retirement income for 6 months.
1 year	13. Begin the process of selling your practice or business.

Worksheet A.4 (*continued*)

6 months	14. Determine which of your assets will be used to provide your retirement income for the first 5 years and which assets are earmarked for legacy, charitable, or long-term purposes.
	15. Investigate your long-term care insurance options and apply for it, if appropriate.
	16. Meet with a retirement plan administrator/ counselor to get more accurate pension plan payout options.
3 months	17. Get a thorough physical exam.
	18. Arrange for health insurance during retirement.
	19. Apply for Social Security and Medicare benefits.
	20. Make arrangements for an extended cruise or other vacation the day after retirement to transition into retirement.
1 month	21. Arrange paperwork for transfer of retirement plan to IRA account, and/or select monthly pension options.
	22. Arrange for tail coverage on professional liability insurance, if appropriate.
	23. Fine-tune your arrangements with your financial advisor, your tax professional, and attorney.
Retirement!	24. ENJOY! Start your journey with a long trip.

The Retirement Readiness Process™ is a trademark of Kelemen Advisory Associates, LLC.
© 2013 Ron Kelemen. PDF form available at www.ConfidentRetirementJourney.com.

Worksheet A.5 Getting started

Sometimes the hardest part of any journey is just getting started. Here's another way of working on the things you need to do for a successful retirement journey and for basic financial planning.

Quick and Easy

- ☐ Make a list of what you think it will take to make this a good year for you personally, professionally, and financially.
- ☐ Get your 401(k) or other retirement plan payroll deduction on track to max out by the end of the year.
- ☐ Set up a 529 College Savings Plan for children, grandchildren, and others.
- ☐ Review your beneficiary designations for retirement accounts, insurance policies, and annuities. (Are they consistent with your wishes and your overall estate plan?)

Easy but Takes More Time

- ☐ Start tracking your expenses.
- ☐ Roll over a retirement plan from a former employer to an existing IRA.
- ☐ Roll over a small IRA into your active retirement plan.
- ☐ Shred unneeded financial records.
- ☐ Fill out the Location of Documents form in the Just in Case worksheet so that if something happened to you, your survivors could easily locate important documents, passwords, safe deposit box keys, etc.
- ☐ Meet with your tax professional for some midyear tax planning.
- ☐ Schedule an update meeting with your financial advisor to review your progress toward key goals.
- ☐ Review the asset allocation and your comfort level with the risk of your portfolio (harder to do on your own, but easier with a financial professional).

Worksheet A.5 (*continued*)

☐ Meet with your property and casualty insurance agent to review potential gaps in your coverage.

☐ Review with your insurance agent your life and disability-income insurance policies for adequacy and sustainability.

☐ Plan a vacation six to twelve months from now.

More Time Involved and Takes More Thought

☐ Engage the services of a financial advisor to learn what your Financial Independence Number is and what it will take to achieve it.

☐ Simplify your financial life by consolidating accounts.

☐ Review and update your estate plan—or get one created!

☐ Set up a qualified retirement plan for your professional practice or business.

☐ Meet with an independent agent to review your options for long-term care.

☐ Think about what it will take over the next ten years for you to feel happy about your personal, professional, and financial progress. Then develop some benchmarks between now and then.

Internet Resources

Here are some websites that provide good information about retirement planning, investing, selecting a financial advisor, and other useful information.

Caregiver information
www.caregiverhelp.com

Certified Financial Planner Board of Standards, Inc.—
The accrediting board for CERTIFIED FINANCIAL PLANNER™ professionals
www.cfp.net
www.letsmakeaplan.org

The Confident Retirement Journey: Your Personal & Financial Road Map—A website containing worksheets, retirement resources, book ordering information, reviews, commentary, and more useful links
www.ConfidentRetirementJourney.com

Digital assets information
www.yourdigitalafterlife.com/resources

Employee Benefit Research Institute—A nonpartisan, nonprofit research organization on retirement issues
www.ebri.org

Financial Industry Regulatory Authority—The largest independent regulator for securities firms
www.finra.org

Financial Planning Association—A multidisciplinary organization of financial advisors
www.fpanet.org

Life-expectancy calculator
www.realage.com

Long-term care costs by region
https://www.genworth.com/corporate/about-genworth/
industry-expertise/cost-of-care.html

Long-term care information
www.longtermcare.gov

Medicare information
www.goodcare.com
www.medicare.gov

National Association of Personal Financial Advisors—
The organization of fee-only comprehensive financial advisors
www.napfa.org

Ron Kelemen's practice and The H Group, Inc.—Websites
with blogs, newsletters, and other resources
www.planningvisionprocess.com
www.thehgroup.com

Social Security
www.socialsecurity.gov

Strategic Coach®—Business and life-planning coaching
for entrepreneurs
www.strategiccoach.com

US Securities and Exchange Commission—An investor-
education site
www.investor.gov

Notes

Introduction

[1] *Worth Magazine,* January 1995.

Chapter 1 The Retirement Landscape

[2] Michael Stein, *The Prosperous Retirement: Guide to the New Reality* (Boulder, CO: EMSTCO Press, 1998).

[3] "Actuarial Tables," IRS, accessed July 25, 2013, http://www.irs.gov/Retirement-Plans/Actuarial-Tables.

[4] Society of Actuaries group Living to 100 Project and Tim Harris, "Understanding Longevity: What to Tell Your Clients" (presentation, NAPFA West Conference, committee on Post Retirement Needs and Risks and the Society of Actuaries Living to 100 Project, Portland, OR, 2012).

[5] "CPI Inflation Calculator, 1976–1999," US Department of Labor Bureau of Labor Statistics, http://www.bls.gov/data/inflation_calculator.htm.

[6] "CPI Inflation Calculator, 1962–2012," US Department of Labor Bureau of Labor Statistics, http://www.bls.gov/data/inflation_calculator.htm.

[7] Jim Shambo, "The Hedonic Pleasure Index: An Enhanced Model for Spending Inflation," *Journal of Financial Planning,* November 2008.

[8] "2013 Annual Report of the Board of Trustees of the Federal Old-Age and Survivors Insurance and Federal Disability Insurance Trust Funds," Social Security Administration, accessed June 5, 2013, http://www.socialsecurity.gov/OACT/TR/2013/.

[9] "Maximum Retirement Benefit," Social Security Administration, accessed August 9, 2013, http://ssa-custhelp.ssa.gov/app/answers/detail/a_id/5/related/1.

[10] "2013 Annual Report of the Board of Trustees," Social Security Administration.

[11] Ibid.

[12] "Fidelity Estimates Couples Retiring in 2013 Will Need $220,000 to Pay Medical Expenses Throughout Retirement," Fidelity.com, accessed May 15, 2013, http://www.fidelity.com/inside-fidelity/individual-investing/fidelity-estimates-couples-

retiring-in-2013-will-need-220000-to-pay-medical-expenses-throughout-retirement.

[13] "Longtermcare.gov: Find Your Path Forward," US Department of Health and Human Services, http://longtermcare.gov.

Chapter 3 Where Are You Now?

[14] Employee Benefit Research Institute and Mathew Greenwald & Associates, Inc., *2013 Retirement Confidence Survey,* http://www.ebri.org/pdf/surveys/rcs/2013/Final-FS.RCS-13.FS_1.Conf.FINAL.pdf.

[15] "Joelle Saad-Lessler and Teresa Ghilarducci, "Fact Sheet Retirement Balances July 2012," Schwartz Center for Economic Policy Analysis-The New School, http://www.economicpolicyresearch.org/index.php/retirement-security.

Chapter 4 What's Your Number?

[16] William Bengen, "Determining Withdrawal Rates Using Historical Data," *Journal of Financial Planning,* October 1994.

[17] Philip L. Cooley, Carl M. Hubbard, and Daniel T. Walz, "Retirement Savings: Choosing a Withdrawal Rate That Is Sustainable," *AAII Journal* 20, no. 2 (February 1998).

[18] Michael Kitces, "What Returns Are Safe Withdrawal Rates Really Based Upon?" *Nerd's Eye View Blog,* August 15, 2012, http://www.kitces.com/index.php.

[19] "Medicare Benefits and Out-of-Pocket Costs in 2013," Goodcare.com, http://www.goodcare.com/downloads/toolkit.

Chapter 5 How Do You Get There?

[20] Mitch Anthony, *The New Retirementality: Planning Your Life and Living Your Dreams at Any Age You Want,* 3rd Ed. (Hoboken, NJ: John Wiley and Sons, 2008).

Chapter 6 Putting Your Financial Independence Assets to Work

[21] "2013 Annual Report of the Board of Trustees," Social Security Administration.

[22] "2013 Annual Report of the Board of Trustees: Figure II.D2.—OASDI Income, Cost, and Expenditures as Percentages of Taxable Payroll," Social Security Administration, http://www.socialsecurity.gov/OACT/TR/2013/II_D_project.html#126461.

[23] Social Security Administration, "Social Security Board of Trustees: No Change in Projected Year of Trust Fund Reserve Depletion," press release, May 13, 2013, http://socialsecurity.gov/pressoffice/pr/trustee13-pr.html.

Chapter 7 Dealing with Detours

[24] "Long-Term Care: Perceptions, Experiences, and Attitudes among Americans 40 or Older," The Associated Press-NORC Center for Public Affairs Research, April 2013, http://www.apnorc.org/projects/Pages/long-term-care-perceptions-experiences-and-attitudes-among-americans-40-or-older.aspx.

[25] "The Basics," US Department of Health and Human Services, http://longtermcare.gov/the-basics/.

[26] Geneworth, *2013 Cost of Care Survey: Home Care Providers, Adult Day Health Care Facilities, Assisted Living Facilities, and Nursing homes,* 10th Ed., https://www.genworth.com/dam/Americas/US/PDFs/Consumer/corporate/131168_031813_Executive%20Summary.pdf.

[27] "How Much Care Will You Need?" US Department of Health and Human Services, http://longtermcare.gov/the-basics/how-much-care-will-you-need/.

[28] Alzheimer's Association, "2012 Alzheimer's Disease Facts and Figures," *Alzheimer's & Dementia* 8, no. 2 (2012).

[29] United States Census Bureau, "More Young Adults Are Living in Their Parents' Home, Census Bureau Reports," press release, November 3, 2011, http://www.census.gov/newsroom/releases/archives/families_households/cb11-183.html.

[30] Jackie Burrell, "Boomerang Kids and Rent: Five Ways to Deal with the Thorny Issue of Rent When Grown Children Move Home," About.com, accessed July 2013, http://youngadults.about.com/od/movinghome/a/Rent.htm.

[31] Investment Company Institute, *2013 Investment Company Fact Book: A Review of Trends and Activities in the US Investment Company Industry,* 53rd ed., http://www.icifactbook.org/pdf/2013_factbook.pdf.

Chapter 8 Beyond the Horizon

[32] Evan Carroll and John Romano, *Your Digital Afterlife: When Facebook, Flickr, and Twitter Are Your Estate, What's Your Legacy?* (Berkeley, CA: New Riders, 2011).

Ron Kelemen

Index